KINDERGARTEN

God Loves Us

AUTHORS
Sisters of Notre Dame
Chardon, Ohio

LOYOLA PRESS.
A JESUIT MINISTRY
Chicago

Nihil Obstat: Reverend Jeffrey S. Grob, S.T.L., J.C.L., Censor Deputatus, November 10, 2006
Imprimatur: Reverend John F. Canary, S.T.L., D. Min., Vicar General, Archdiocese of Chicago, December 1, 2006

The *Nihil Obstat* and *Imprimatur* are official declarations that a book is free of doctrinal and moral error. No implication is contained therein that those who have granted the *Nihil Obstat* and *Imprimatur* agree with the content, opinions, or statements expressed. Nor do they assume any legal responsibility associated with publication.

God Loves Us of the
God Made Everything Series
found to be in conformity

The Ad Hoc Committee to Oversee the Use of the Catechism, United States Conference of Catholic Bishops, has found this pre-school series, copyright 2008, to be in conformity with the *Catechism of the Catholic Church.*

Acknowledgments for Kindergarten *God Loves Us* Student Book

Excerpts from the *New American Bible* with Revised New Testament and Psalms Copyright © 1991, 1986, 1970 Confraternity of Christian Doctrine, Inc., Washington, DC. All rights reserved. No portion of the *New American Bible* may be reprinted without permission in writing from the copyright holder.

Excerpts from the English translation of *The Roman Missal* © 2010, International Commission on English in the Liturgy Corporation (ICEL). All rights reserved.

Unless otherwise acknowledged, photos are the property of Loyola Press. When there is more than one picture on a page, credits are supplied in sequence, left to right, top to bottom. Page positions are abbreviated as follows: (t) top, (c) center, (b) bottom, (l) left, (r) right.

Illustration

Cheryl Arnemann: 49, 88, 93, 96
Nan Brooks: 2, 3, 23, 48, 85, 119, 128
Robert Crawford: 37
Martin Erspamer, OSB.: 111
Laura Fry: 104–105
Susan Tolonen: 6, 7, 44, 45, 54, 55, 108, 110
Yoshi Miyake: 113, 117, 131, 137
Mike Muir: 11, 15, 59, 133
Eileen Mueller Neill & Kelly Neill: 127
Proof Positive/Farrowlyne Assoc., Inc.: 123
Ida Pearl: 32
Robert Voigts: 75, 81, 89, 97

Photography

UNIT 1: 1 Mike Timo/Stone/Getty Images. **4**(tl)Jose Ortega/ Stock Illustration Source/Getty Images. **6**(tr) Camille Tokerud/ Photographer's Choice/Getty Images. **8** Stephanie Howard/Stone/ Getty Images. **8**(tr) © The Crosiers/Gene Plaisted OSC. **9**(b) Christoph Wilhelm/Taxi/Getty Images. **10** David Young-Wolff/Photographer's Choice/Getty Images. **10**(tl) © The Crosiers/Gene Plaisted OSC. **14**(tl) Aaron Graubart/Iconica/Getty Images. **14**(tr) Altrendo/Altrendo Images/Getty Images. **18**(tr) Eri Morita/Stone/Getty Images. **18**(tlc) PIER/Stone/Getty Images. **19**(tr) Camille Tokerud/The Image Bank/ Getty Images. **22**(b) Ariel Skelley/CORBIS. **24**(tr) Kevin Hatt/ Photonica/Getty Images. **27**(trl) © The Crosiers/Gene Plaisted OSC. **28**(br) © The Crosiers/Gene Plaisted OSC.

29(tr) © The Crosiers/Gene Plaisted OSC. **30**(tr) © The Crosiers/Gene Plaisted OSC. **31** Altrendo/Altrendo Images/Getty Images. **35**(br) Randy Faris/CORBIS. **35**(tl) © The Crosiers/Gene Plaisted OSC. **36**(b) Dave Nagel/Taxi/Getty Images. **43** Yellow Dog Productions/ The Image Bank/Getty Images. **47** Karen Kapoor/Taxi/Getty Images. **50**(tl) © The Crosiers/Gene Plaisted OSC. **51**(bl) Mark Hall/ Photonica/Getty Images. **53** Ronnie Kaufman/CORBIS. **56**(tr) © The Crosiers/Gene Plaisted OSC. **57** Anne-Marie Weber/CORBIS. **58** Ariel Skelley/CORBIS. **60**(tl) © The Crosiers/Gene Plaisted OSC. **61** © Mark Grimberg/Getty Images. **62** © The Crosiers/Gene Plaisted OSC. **63**(tc) bread & butter/Photographer's Choice/Getty Images. **63**(tl) Elyse Lewin/Photographer's Choice/Getty Images. **65** Grace/ zefa/CORBIS. **67** © The Crosiers/Gene Plaisted OSC. **72**(tr) © The Crosiers/Gene Plaisted OSC. **73**(t) © The Crosiers/Gene Plaisted OSC. **73**(b) Andersen Ross/Getty Images. **77**(lc) © The Crosiers/Gene Plaisted OSC. **81**(tr) Phil Martin Photography. **83** Steven Puetzer/ Solus Photography/Veer. **84**(lc) Phil Martin Photography. **84**(tr) © The Crosiers/Gene Plaisted OSC. **87** Peter Rodger/Workbook Stock/ Getty Images. **90**(tr) © The Crosiers/Gene Plaisted OSC. **92**(tl) © Bill Wittman Photography. **92**(br) Agnus Images. **94**(tr) Phil Martin Photography. **95** Mark Gamba/CORBIS. **96** © The Crosiers/Gene Plaisted OSC. **97**(tr) © The Crosiers/Gene Plaisted OSC. **98**(cr) © The Crosiers/Gene Plaisted OSC. **99** Joe McBride/Taxi/Getty Images. **100**(tc) Siri Stafford/Stone/Getty Images. **100**(bc) Emmanuel Faure/ Taxi/Getty Images. **101**(br) Joe Polillio/Photographer's Choice/Getty Images. **101**(tl) © The Crosiers/Gene Plaisted OSC. **102**(tr) © The Crosiers/Gene Plaisted OSC. **107**(cl) Phil Martin Photography. **107**(cr) © The Crosiers/Gene Plaisted OSC. **112**(br) Gary Gay/Photographer's Choice/Getty Images. **113**(tl) Annie Engel/zefa/CORBIS. **114**(br) © The Crosiers/Gene Plaisted OSC. **115**(tl) © Bill Wittman Photography. **116**(tr) © Bill Wittman Photography. **119**(tr) © The Crosiers/Gene Plaisted OSC. **120**(l) © The Crosiers/Gene Plaisted OSC. **121**(tr) © The Crosiers/Gene Plaisted OSC. **122**(tr) © The Crosiers/Gene Plaisted OSC. **123**(tr) © The Crosiers/Gene Plaisted OSC. **124**(tr) © The Crosiers/Gene Plaisted OSC. **125**(trl) © The Crosiers/Gene Plaisted OSC. **126**(br) © Bill Wittman Photography. **127**(tr) © The Crosiers/ Gene Plaisted OSC. **128**(br) © Office Central de Lisieux. **129**(tr) © The Crosiers/Gene Plaisted OSC. **130**(tl) © The Crosiers/Gene Plaisted OSC. **131**(tr) © The Crosiers/Gene Plaisted OSC. **132**(bl) Paul C. Pet/ zefa/CORBIS. **133**(tr) © The Crosiers/Gene Plaisted OSC. **134**(tl) © The Crosiers/Gene Plaisted OSC. **135**(tr) © The Crosiers/Gene Plaisted OSC. **136** Courtesy Sisters of Notre Dame **137**(tl) © The Crosiers/Gene Plaisted OSC. **138**(tr) © The Crosiers/Gene Plaisted OSC.

Design: Loyola Press, Judine O'Shea
Cover Art: Susan Tolonen

ISBN 10: 0-8294-2401-6, ISBN 13: 978-0-8294-2401-0

For more information related to the English translation of the *Roman Missal, Third Edition,* see www.loyolapress.com/romanmissal.

Dedicated to St. Julie Billiart, foundress of the Sisters of Notre Dame, in gratitude for her inspiration and example

LOYOLAPRESS.
A JESUIT MINISTRY

3441 N. Ashland Avenue
Chicago, Illinois 60657
(800) 621-1008
www.loyolapress.com

Webcrafters, Inc. / Madison, WI, USA / 03-15 / 8th Printing

God Loves Us

UNIT 4 CELEBRATING GOD'S LOVE

SPECIAL SEASONS AND DAYS · · · · · 109

As parents, you have a sacred trust. You are the primary religious educators of your child. God calls you to nurture not only the physical life of your child but also the life of grace he or she received at Baptism. This responsibility requires that you grow in your own faith and that you share your faith with your family. Here are some steps to deepen your relationship with God and with your family this year:

- Set aside a time (about 15 minutes) and a quiet place for private prayer each day. Read the Bible, Bible commentaries, or spiritual books, and listen to the Lord speak to you. Respond to him.

- Set aside a time for family prayer each day, preferably at mealtimes.

- Celebrate the Eucharist on Sundays or Saturday evenings as a family, if possible. Children learn much from your example of prayer.

- Make reconciliation, forgiving and being forgiven, a part of family living. Celebrate the Sacrament of Reconciliation (Penance) regularly.

- Attend adult faith formation programs scheduled in your parish.

- Involve your whole family in service projects for the Church and civic community.

- Proudly live out your faith at home, at work, in the neighborhood, and in the world.

In addition to experiencing God's love in your family, your child will learn more about his love through the religious education program.

The first-semester kindergarten program, God Loves Us, is designed to make the children aware of God's love through the many good and beautiful persons, events, and things he has placed in their lives. Each chapter leads the children to appreciate their uniqueness and to sense God's presence in all the wonderful things around them.

The second-semester kindergarten program, We Love God, continues the themes of the first semester. It also leads the children to a greater desire to love God in return through their prayers and acts of kindness for others.

The family page of your child's book, located on the last page of each chapter, briefs you on what your child learned in class and offers suggestions for living the message in your family. Since the children's text contains the message, you are encouraged to read it over with your child each week. However, it is advisable not to read chapters to your child until after they have been presented in class. Each unit ends with family feature pages to further nurture your faith and to provide activities to do at home.

The reverse side of this page lists 10 ways that you can nurture your child's faith. Post it on your refrigerator or keep this list handy where you will see it in the course of your day.

May God continue to bless you and your family, and, in the words of Saint Paul, "may he give you the power through his Spirit for your hidden self to grow strong, so that Christ may live in your hearts through faith." (Based on Ephesians 3:16)

Ten Principles to Nurture Your Child's Faith

1. Listen with your heart as well as with your head.

2. Encourage wonder and curiosity in your child.

3. Coach your child in empathy early. It's a building block for morality.

4. Display religious artwork in your home. This will serve as a steady witness that faith is an important part of life.

5. Gently guide your child to a life of honesty.

6. Whenever appropriate, model for your child how to say, "I'm sorry."

7. Eat meals together regularly as a family. It will be an anchor for your child in days to come.

8. Pray together in good times and bad. Worship regularly together as a family.

9. Be generous to those who need help. Make helping others an important focus of your life as a family.

10. See your child for the wonder that God made. Communicate your conviction that your child was created for a noble purpose—to serve God and others in this life and to be happy with God forever in the next.

Welcomes Are Good

Jesus welcomed little children.

Ni hao

Hello

Buenos Días

Bonjour

Jambo

Scripture

He said, "Let the children come to me."
Based on Mark 10:14

Jesus loves children.

Jesus welcomes us.

He wants us to know him.

Jesus loves us.

Others welcome us.
We welcome others.

 Try This

Look at the pictures of people showing welcome.

Circle them.

Think about how you might welcome others today.

Welcomes in Families

The Lesson Your Child Learned

When we welcome other people, we also welcome Jesus into our lives. In this chapter, the children were encouraged to reach out to others and make them feel welcome. They learned that Jesus loves and welcomes children and that he wants them to know him.

Living the Lesson

Can you recall your first day on a new job or at a new school? How about the first time you met your prospective in-laws? Do you recall how awkward everything seemed until someone made you feel welcome? You can probably still remember the people who first made you feel at home in those situations.

Hospitality, the act of welcoming others and making a place for them, is not only good manners; it's a religious act as well. Jesus made it very clear that those who fed the hungry, gave drink to the thirsty, and welcomed the stranger were, in fact, caring for and welcoming Jesus himself.

This week, think about the welcomes you give and the welcomes you receive. Pay particular attention to how welcome you make your child feel, especially when life is busy and you are facing many demands. Realize that the first gift we're meant to give the children in our care is to receive them well—as the unique and wonderful people God made them.

–Tom McGrath, author of *Raising Faith-Filled Kids* (Loyola Press)

Bringing the Lesson Home

- Ask your child to tell you what he or she learned this week. Read with your child the pages that were sent home. Go over the activity on the back of this page together.

- Children learn hospitality by modeling the acts of welcoming they observe among adults. As parents, we teach these things because we wish to teach our children good manners. Hospitality is about manners, and it is also a Christian value. Take advantage of opportunities to teach your child to greet visitors politely and to offer simple gestures of hospitality, such as taking coats and inviting guests to be seated.

CHAPTER 2

Names Are Good

Who Are You?

I'm Anna!

When our friends call us by name, we feel good.

My name is

Jesus is God.

His name is holy.

We say Jesus' name with love.

God tells us his name.

He loves us.

Scripture

At the name of Jesus every knee should bend. Based on Philippians 2:9–10

Jesus' name is holy.
Color the letters in Jesus' name.

JeSuS

Names in Families

The Lesson Your Child Learned

To pronounce the name of Jesus reverently is to show respect for him. In this chapter the children talked about the importance of names. They were led to experience the mystery of God by becoming aware that Jesus' name is holy.

Living the Lesson

You may have seen that running gag on the TV show *Seinfeld*. Every time Jerry ran into the irritating neighbor who lived upstairs, he would sneer his name, "Newman," in the same way you might talk about a dreaded disease. That one word spoke volumes about Jerry's negative feelings. It was a recurring example of how the way we use names reveals what's in our hearts.

We should be careful with the names we use and how we use them. Every one of us longs for respect. We can offer that respect to those in our family as a way of recognizing that we are all made in the image of God. One of the surest ways to show respect is to say one another's names with kindness and care—even when we are angry!

There was an e-mail going around the Internet a few years ago listing the responses of young children to the question, "How would you define the word love?" One five-year-old reportedly said, "When somebody loves you, your name is safe in their mouth." To take this week's lesson to heart, make sure the names of your family members are "safe in your mouth" and show the same care for the names we use for God.

–Tom McGrath, author of *Raising Faith-Filled Kids* (Loyola Press)

Bringing the Lesson Home

- Read with your child the pages that were sent home.

- Share with your child the significance of his or her name—its meaning and why it was chosen. If the name was given to honor a family member or friend, tell about the qualities of that person that you admire. Encourage your child to greet by name the people he or she meets.

- Talk with your child about nicknames. Tell your child that nicknames are welcome and fun only if the person likes the name he or she is being called. Explain that one of the first things bullies usually do is give mean names to the kids they want to bully—and that is wrong.

- Some families make a practice of bowing their head slightly whenever they use the name of Jesus. This is something your family might like to do as a sign of respect for our Lord.

- Pray Psalm 8:2 as part of your family prayers this week. Ask your child to teach you and other family members the gestures for this psalm and pray it together as a family.

CHAPTER 3

Stories Are Good

Books are full of stories.
Stories can make us laugh or cry,
open wide our eyes with wonder,
or even shout with joy.

The Bible is a holy book.

It tells the story of God's love for us.

The Bible tells the story of Jesus.

He came to show us God's love.

God's people listen to his story.

Scripture

We will tell the wonderful things the Lord has done.

Based on Psalm 78:4

A Bible Story

1

Jonah runs away from God.

2

A storm comes.

3

A whale swallows Jonah.

4

Jonah lands where God wants him.

5

He preaches and people listen.

6

God loves all people.

The Bible in Families

The Lesson Your Child Learned

God reveals himself to us whenever the Bible is read. When we listen or read with faith, we are led to understand God's action working in our lives—calling us to commit ourselves to him. The children learned that the Bible, which contains Jesus' story, is a holy book that tells about God's love for us. They also learned that God's people listen to readings from the Bible at Mass.

Living the Lesson

People love stories. We read them. We watch them in theaters and on television. We listen to them on the radio and on our iPods. We tell stories when we're gathered around water coolers, kitchen tables, and campfires. And we recall them when extended-family members get together. Our family stories often carry within them deep beliefs about who we are and what we value. The same is true with the Bible, which is a collection of stories and accounts of how God created us and acted throughout history to save us from bondage to sin. The Bible tells us who we are (God's own beloved children) and what we value (faithfulness, forgiveness, and generosity, to name a few). It tells us where we came from (the heart of God), where we are going (to live with God for all eternity), and how we will get there (by loving God and our fellow human beings and by following God's ways).

–Tom McGrath, author of *Raising Faith-Filled Kids* (Loyola Press)

Bringing the Lesson Home

- Encourage your child to tell you about what he or she has learned. Talk about the class activities, which included having the children tell about themselves. Read with your child the pages that were sent home.

- Together with your child, choose a place of honor in your home where you will keep your family Bible. Have your child place it reverently in the spot you choose. Invite your child to tell about God's message of love to us in the Bible.

- Begin reading short, appropriate sections of the Bible (or *A Child's Bible*) to your child. You might choose Mark 10:13–16, Jeremiah 31:3, and parts of Genesis 1.

- Use Psalm 78:4 as a prayer before reading from the Bible. Invite your child to teach you the gestures for this psalm, which the children prayed during this week.

CHAPTER 4

God's World Is Good

Blue skies
Spotted giraffes
Hoppity rabbits
Puddles to splash.

Red-ripe apples
Trees to climb
Sandy beaches
Shells to find.

Green grass
Tickling my toes
People with hugs
A baby that grows.

**God made this
wonderful
world!**

God gave the world to us.

God wants us to care for it.

The Bible tells us so.

All the good things in the world tell us about God.

They tell us that God loves us.

Scripture

The earth is full of the goodness of the Lord. Based on Psalm 33:5

In the Bible God made a promise to Noah. God promised to always love everything on earth. The rainbow is a sign of God's love.

Try This

1. Find the animals in the clouds. Circle them.

2. Say thank you to God for the beautiful things he made.

Creation in Families

The Lesson Your Child Learned

All creation speaks of God's glory and love for us. When we look around, we can see God's handiwork. Everything that God created is good, and through the works of creation, we know God better. In this chapter the children were led to see how the wonderful works of creation show us God's goodness and love. They were encouraged to respond to God's love by caring for the world God made.

Living the Lesson

I used to ride the "El," Chicago's elevated train, on my way to college classes. We passed through some neighborhoods that were on the decline, traveling alongside once-grand apartment buildings that had seen better days. One year as winter moved tentatively into spring, one of the apartment dwellers planted a window box with flowers. As the days went by, the plants grew and the flowers blossomed, offering a sign of hope to passersby. Soon other neighbors put out their own window boxes, proving that a touch of nature—even in such small doses as a window box full of flowers—can be healing and transforming.

There are a number of spiritual lessons to be learned from time spent appreciating God's creation. The wonders of nature can teach us that all creation is connected, that dying often leads to new and abundant life, and that having "enough" is better than constantly craving more. But perhaps the best reason to spend time cultivating an appreciation of nature is that doing so helps us develop our capacity to notice the subtle signs of God's action in our own lives. Nature helps us become attuned to mystery and thus to the reality that there is more going on in the world than first meets the eye. There are wonders all around us if only we will awaken to them.

–Tom McGrath, author of *Raising Faith-Filled Kids* (Loyola Press)

Bringing the Lesson Home

- Encourage your child to tell you about what he or she has learned this week. Read with your child the pages that were sent home.

- To help your family stay more attuned to your surroundings, create your own litany. Have each of your family members pick out something they observe and say, for example, "For that tall tree," to which everyone else responds, "Praise the Lord."

- Let your child participate in a recycling program in your area or work in your garden. Your child will learn responsibility and various ways to respond to God's call to care for the earth.

- Pray Psalm 33:5 as part of your family prayers this week. Invite your child to lead your family as you pray this together.

- Read aloud Genesis 1:31 and appropriate sections from Psalms 65, 66, and 104.

CHAPTER 5

Quiet Is Good

Quiet is clouds moving across the sky,
a loving hug and a friendly smile,
yellow butterflies dancing in the sun,
green grass growing in the yard,
a warm and happy feeling deep inside,
SHH-SHH-SHH.

Scripture

Be still and know that I am God.
Based on Psalm 46:11

Quiet helps us enter into our hearts.
We meet God there.

God is also with us
in a special way in church.

God loves us.

Quiet helps us think of God.
It helps us love God.

Try This

Look at the pictures showing quiet times that help you think of God.

Circle them.

Think of God. Remember how much God loves you.

Quiet in Families

The Lesson Your Child Learned

Silence helps us enter into our innermost selves and encounter God present within us. In this chapter the children learned that good and beautiful things happen in quiet. Through a guided reflection, they learned how to meet God present within them.

Living the Lesson

One year I gave up listening to the radio in the car for Lent, and it was one of the hardest things I've ever done. The first lesson it taught me was how noisy my mind was. The second lesson was how I used

outside entertainment to drown out those noises in my head. But eventually, after a time of withdrawal, I began to appreciate the silence and found it possible to enter into silent prayer. I benefited from those quiet times so much that even now I will occasionally turn off the radio or CD player in my car and treat myself to the gift of silence.

I suspect that many people who commit to adding more prayer to their lives also find it difficult at first to quiet both mind and heart. They may erroneously conclude that they are no good at praying and let the opportunity slip away. But even the saints had the same struggles with prayer. It's just that they didn't stop praying when the going got tough. When your intention is right, even calming yourself for prayer is a kind of prayer in itself.

Silence may be an acquired taste, but the rewards are beyond measure. As Father Thomas Keating, O.C.S.O., says, "Silence is God's first language." Why not give yourself the chance to listen in?

–Tom McGrath, author of *Raising Faith-Filled Kids* (Loyola Press)

Bringing the Lesson Home

- Encourage your child to tell about his or her prayer experiences this week. Read with your child the pages that were sent home.

- When your family prays together before meals, introduce a short time for quiet personal prayer and reflection. This form of prayer is more easily modeled than taught. And though it may seem awkward at first, this form of prayer will become more comfortable with practice.

- Encourage your child to enjoy quiet time, either time spent alone or with others. If your child seems anxious or crabby, a short time of quiet and less stimulation may be just what he or she needs. This is not to be confused with punishment; it's merely providing what the child needs at the time.

- If you have not already done so, create a prayer center in your home for quiet and for prayer. A favorite chair or a corner of a room can be designated as a place for prayer and peace.

CHAPTER 6

Talking to God Is Good

We like to talk to those we love:

"Dad, I love you very much."

"Look at the pretty butterflies."

"Thank you for letting me play."

"I'll try to do my best today."

We can talk to God.

We can say, "I love you."

"Thank you, God."

"Please help me do my best today."

God always listens. **God loves us.**

Scripture

"Speak, Lord, for your servant is listening." Based on 1 Samuel 3:10

When we talk to God, we pray. **God bless . . .**

 **Try This**

Finish the prayer. Draw a circle around the people you want to pray for.

Remember that you can talk to God anytime.

You can pray to God in different ways.

Prayer in Families

The Lesson Your Child Learned

Through prayer we encounter God and converse with him as we would with a close friend. Prayer will become part of your child's life when it is an evident part of yours. In this chapter the children learned that prayer can include reflection, speech, gestures, music, song, and dance. They participated in a variety of prayer experiences.

Living the Lesson

Probably the most powerful lesson in prayer I ever received was looking out from the sacristy on my first day as an altar boy. I could see the people gathering for the 6:30 A.M. Mass, and in the front pew I saw my father with his head bowed, lost in prayer. Here the man I viewed as the most powerful guy in the world was on his knees before God. Growing up, I had no doubt that prayer was important to my parents, and as a result I grew up knowing I could always turn to God in every situation of my life. Realize that your example is a powerful way to influence your child's prayer life.

You don't have to be an expert to pray. Your prayer can be as simple as uttering the words, "God, help!" during a tough situation at work or "Thank you, God," when a sick child returns to health. "Prayer is the raising of one's mind and heart to God," says the *Catechism of the Catholic Church.* So raise your heart and your mind regularly. God will be so happy to hear from you.

–Tom McGrath, author of *Raising Faith-Filled Kids* (Loyola Press)

Bringing the Lesson Home

- Encourage your child to tell you about the different ways the class prayed to God. Read with your child the pages that were sent home.

- Let your child see you at prayer and hear you call upon God in times of joy and sorrow.

- Create a prayer jar so that family members can write their names or needs on slips of paper and put them in the jar. Then during the week each person takes out a slip of paper and prays for the other person's needs.

- Decide on a regular time for daily family prayer. Many find mealtimes and bedtime to be good times for family prayer.

- If you have family prayer in a designated prayer center, you might choose to light a candle during prayer.

- When a disaster is reported widely in the news, make a point of praying together as a family for those affected.

Growing Family Faith

The Power of Prayer

Few things are as essential to our health and well-being, yet carry as vast an assortment of experience (and therefore baggage), as prayer. Some of us were never taught how to pray. For others, what was taught wasn't meaningful, so we have placed prayers and praying in a box on a shelf in the back of the closet, to be taken out only on special occasions—at funerals, for example, or when a loved one is ill.

Many of us do use prayer more or less regularly, but we aren't sure what we're doing is right. As one parent lamented, "I keep thinking there must be something like a 'secret handshake' that would make my prayers more effective, but I don't know what it is—or how to find out."

Whatever your experience of prayer is or has been, consider this: Prayer is, at its heart, a remembering. We pray in order to remember who we are. We pray to remember God who is both our source and the eternal essence within each of us that is whole, perfect, and unchanging.

Whether we have been praying all our lives or are just taking the first few tentative steps toward remembering who we are, let us take encouragement from the Trappist monk Thomas Merton, who observed, "We do not want to be beginners, but let us be convinced that we will never be anything else but beginners all our life."

If prayer is not yet a part of your daily life, the good news is that it's never too late to begin! Here are a few old and new ideas to try alone or with your family:

Putting More Prayer in Your Day

- Create a regular time and a place to pray. Plan to wake up 30 minutes earlier every morning, or take 20 minutes of your lunch hour, or commit to a prayer time before you go to sleep each night. Experiment until you find the time and place that you are least likely to be interrupted.

- Find a book of prayers that you like and use it daily. There are hundreds of them on the market, or you may already have one at home.

- If you prayed as a child, revisit some of the prayers you prayed then. You have a different perspective now that you are a parent, and these prayers may resonate in ways they did not when you were younger. For example, see **The Practicing Catholic** on page 26. Pray these prayers with your child and tell why they mean so much to you.

- Create a simple ritual that you and your child could perform at the beginning or end of each day.

Putting More Prayer in Your Day *continued*

Try reading these two lines from Psalm 118:24 each morning:

Adult: *This is the day the Lord has made…*

Child: *Let us rejoice and be glad.*

- Before you begin any prayer, ask your child if there is anyone for whom he or she would like to pray. Then be sure to add your own intention. This simple exercise teaches children to think of others and reminds them that prayer benefits even those who are not present.

- Check out bookstores, the Internet, or your local library for a book of mealtime prayers to use each time you and your child share a meal together.

- Take your child to Mass with you each week. The Mass, of course, is *the* prayer, the great remembering of who we are and who we aspire to be. If your child reacts negatively, have your response ready: "This is who we are. This is what we do."

- Write your prayer in the form of a letter to God each prayer time. At first this might seem like an impossible undertaking, but the inspiration, peace, and comfort it provides make it an exercise that will become a joyful, life-giving habit. Try it, you'll like it!

The Practicing Catholic

During the Vietnam War, my father decided that our family would pray the Rosary together every night for three years while my brother was in the Marines. My brother came home safely, but by then I was pretty sure I never wanted to say another Rosary again! Recently though, I had the idea to time my morning stretching exercises by saying the Our Father and the Hail Mary instead of counting the seconds. After a week I realized I had an entire Rosary in my exercise routine. This simple change has transformed my experience of both prayer and exercise. It also connects me in a profound way to my father, who died over ten years ago.

—Ann O'Connor, author of *The Twelve Unbreakable Principles of Parenting*
(ACTA Publications)

We cannot find God in noise or agitation. Nature: trees, flowers, and grass grow in silence. The stars, the moon, and the sun move in silence.   —Mother Teresa

Families Are Good

God made us to belong to families. Family members love and care for one another.

Jesus lived with Mary and Joseph. They are called the Holy Family.

In God, we are brothers and sisters to people all over the world.

When we were baptized we became part of God's special family, the Church.

The pope in Rome is the leader of the Church.

God is our Father. He loves us and watches over us. We pray,

Scripture

"Our Father, who art in heaven, hallowed be thy name."

Based on Matthew 6:9

We belong to God's family.
We are his children. **God is our Father.**

Try This

1. Draw lines to show to which family each one belongs.

2. Pray for people all over the world. They are your brothers and sisters.

God's Love in Families

The Lesson Your Child Learned

Jesus reveals that God is the Father of us all and that we are to be as brothers and sisters in his family. The children learned that all members contribute to making a happy family. They learned that in God, they are brothers and sisters to people all over the world. Through their Baptism, they are members of God's family, the Church, and call God "Father." They were introduced to the first two lines of the Our Father. Place the Our Father prayer card your child brought home in a special place of honor.

Living the Lesson

My most vivid image of family is when a dozen of my cousins and I crammed into a side bedroom at my grandparents' house on Thanksgiving. There wasn't enough room for all us kids at the big dining room table and so we had our own private dining room, where we laughed and told stories and got to know one another, even the cousins who lived far away.

Now whenever we gather, whether it's joyously at a wedding or solemnly at a funeral, we share memories of Thanksgiving dinners tucked away in one of Grandma's extra bedrooms. That's where we learned some fundamental life lessons we'll never forget: everyone belongs at the table; we'll always be family; we are loved; and it is gratitude that brings us together. Whether yours is a large, raucous family or just a few who gather around your table, families are meant to be gifts. When a family is healthy, loving, nurturing, and forgiving, it reflects the loving community of the Trinity.

–Tom McGrath, author of *Raising Faith-Filled Kids* (Loyola Press)

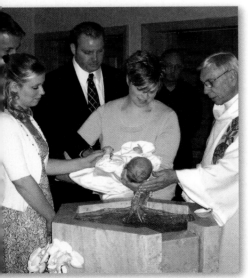

Bringing the Lesson Home

- Read with your child the pages that were sent home.

- Children grow physically, psychologically, and spiritually when they know that they are loved. The signs of affection that you share with your child and with other family members help to strengthen each one's sense of well-being. These also help to strengthen the bonds between all family members.

- Show your child pictures of his or her Baptism.

- Declare and celebrate a special Family Week. Select a different member to honor at the family meal each day. Take turns telling the honored member about what makes him or her special and about how important he or she is to your family.

- Pray the Our Father together each day as a family.

CHAPTER 8

I Am Good

Henry

Hey, wake me! Wake me!
Time to walk
Listening for the flowers' talk!
See me! See me!
Wrinkling my nose,
Smelling a rose.
Me! Me! Wrinkle-nose,
wonderful me!

Swing me! Push me!
Way up high.
I need to get me
a piece of sky.

Catch me! Catch me!
Here I come
Zooming right into
your open arms.

Feed me! Feed me!
I'm weak in the knees.
Some peanut butter
and jelly, please.

Hold me! Hold me!
Squeeze me tight.
Now's the time
to kiss good night.

Me! Me!
Sleepyhead,
wonderful
me!

I can do all kinds of wonderful things.

I thank God for making wonderful ME.

God made me wonderful.

God made me.

God loves me.

Scripture

I thank you, O Lord, for the wonder
of myself.   Based on Psalm 139:14

I am good. God made me wonderful.

I can hear.

I can taste.

I can touch.

I can smell.

Read the words and look at the pictures.

Make an X on each picture that does not belong.

Thank God for making you so wonderful.

Self Concept in Families

The Lesson Your Child Learned

We are made in God's image and are called to share eternal life with him. In this chapter the children learned that God made them and considers them very precious. They engaged in activities designed to help them appreciate themselves as worthwhile persons.

Living the Lesson

Can you think of a significant person from your younger years who paid you a compliment that stuck with you? Someone you respected who told you something about yourself that gave you a sense of your self-worth? Maybe it was a boss on your first job, a coach who noticed your drive and commitment, or a favorite relative who saw something special in you.

We all need "mirrors" in our life, that is, people who can see us and reflect our goodness back to us. Our children need that positive mirroring from us as well as from others who care about them. They also need the opportunity to use their talents and skills, as well as to exercise their virtue. I'm not talking about giving manufactured compliments to artificially build up their self-esteem. The best way to gain self-esteem is to do "esteem-able" things.

So make a point of observing your child and mirroring back the good you see in him or her. And be sure to offer (and model) a variety of opportunities for your child to take virtuous and worthy action.

–Tom McGrath, author of *Raising Faith-Filled Kids* (Loyola Press)

Bringing the Lesson Home

• Read with your child the pages that were sent home.

• Encourage the members of your family to note and acknowledge one another's successes. Reinforce the importance of sending positive, encouraging messages.

• Children learn by doing. Refrain from helping your child before it is needed. This shows you have trust in your child's abilities and encourages his or her independence and development. Caregivers who rush in to do for their children what they can do for themselves or for others take away a golden opportunity for their children to learn independence as well as the value of contributing to the well-being of the family.

• Let family members make their own decisions whenever possible. Caregivers may worry about what decisions their child will make in the future. But if you give your child the gift of making small and relevant decisions now, your child will have the benefit of learning through consequences on small matters, such as what clothes to wear. As your child grows, the importance of the decisions will grow, and so will his or her ability to make wise choices.

• Show respect and appreciation for the work of each family member.

CHAPTER 9

Growing Is Good

Birds grow. Pumpkins grow.
Elephants grow. Seeds grow. We grow.

bird	pumpkin	young elephant	seedling	You
5 inches	17 inches	84 inches	6 inches	? inches

We grow **bigger**
and **bigger**
and **bigger**.

We keep
growing all
our lives.

We were baptized.
We became members of the Catholic Church.
We became a part of God's family.
We grow in Jesus' love.

We grow more like Jesus.
God our Father loves us.

Draw more branches, leaves, and flowers on the tree to show that it is growing.

Tell God you want to grow to be more like Jesus.

Tell Jesus you will spread his love everywhere.

Scripture

I am like a green olive tree growing before the Lord.   Based on Psalm 52:10

Growing in Families

The Lesson Your Child Learned

Our growth is a lifelong process consisting of never-ending struggles, achievements, and new challenges. Baptism is the beginning of a new way of life, and with the help of the Holy Spirit we can grow into the likeness of Christ. Choosing Baptism for your child indicated your commitment to fostering his or her Christian growth. In this chapter the children learned that at Baptism they became members of the Church.

Living the Lesson

In the house where I grew up, we had a spot alongside our back doorway where Mom and Dad would measure the height of my brother and me every year on our birthdays. When Dad would paint that room, he'd always leave that strip unpainted so the record of our growth would remain visible. The day we moved from that house, I took one last look at all the empty rooms. I recall seeing those penciled lines, with our initials and the dates next to them, and they represented all the good times we'd had together in that home, as well as all the things my brother and I had learned about life, about family, and about ourselves.

Growth means life. Jesus said, "I came so that they might have life and have it more abundantly." (John 10:10) Your child is at a wondrous moment in his or her growth, and you get the privilege of witnessing this miracle as it unfolds. Make sure to stop once in a while and pay attention to how far your child has come and how many wondrous opportunities lie ahead. And don't forget to mark your own growth now and again. Take stock of how you measure up physically, intellectually, emotionally, and spiritually. Are you taking Jesus up on his offer of having life more abundantly?

–Tom McGrath, author of *Raising Faith-Filled Kids* (Loyola Press)

Bringing the Lesson Home

- Read with your child the pages that were sent home.

- Take out your child's baby book and recall some growing-up stories with your child.

- Look at old family pictures so that your child learns that everyone grows and changes—even mommies, daddies, and grandparents.

- Tell your child why you decided to have him or her baptized. Share memories of this day.

- Spend a moment in prayer together, inviting your child to feel God's love. Talk about ways your child can share that good feeling by showing love and kindness to others.

CHAPTER 10

Thanking Is Good

On Thanksgiving Day, we say thank you with a special meal.

We hear and say the words thank you every day.

The words thank you tell people how we feel.

Saying thank you makes people happy.

Father, We Thank You

For flowers that bloom about our feet,
Father, we thank you.
For tender grass so fresh and sweet,
Father, we thank you.
For songs of birds and humming of bees,
For all things fair we hear or see,
Father in heaven, we thank you.

Author Unknown

We thank God for many gifts.
Thank you, God.

Think about the gifts that God gives you.

Draw a circle around the pictures of God's gifts.

Thank God for these wonderful gifts.

Scripture

Always be thankful.

Based on Colossians 3:15–17

Thanksgiving in Families

The Lesson Your Child Learned

In giving thanks to God, we acknowledge that all things have been created by him, belong to him, and come to us through his goodness. Thanksgiving provides an occasion for families to reflect and to express gratitude.

Mealtime is a daily opportunity to pray together. In this chapter the children talked about special times when we thank God. They discovered that thank-yous are for every day. They began to memorize the traditional grace before meals and colored a prayer card for their tables at home as a reminder to pray grace. In a prayer celebration they thanked God for their blessings.

Living the Lesson

In Moline, Illinois, Deacon Tom Vogelbaugh is known as "Mr. Thanksgiving." Years ago he owned a small grocery store in town, and he was moved by the fact that many of his regular customers had no one with whom to celebrate Thanksgiving. So he hosted a dinner for about a dozen such people that year. The idea took off, and the feast grew year after year. Recently, with the help of more than four hundred volunteers, Vogelbaugh served two thousand guests. Over the years he's served up more than 40,000 Thanksgiving meals. When asked why he does this, Vogelbaugh points to his own sense of gratitude for all that people—and God—have done for him through the years.

Gratitude is a fundamental building block of all spirituality. Cultivate an attitude of gratitude, and you will have the eyes to see God's gifts all around you. One of the best gifts we can give our children is the habit of being thankful for the life that we share as a family. And the first step in teaching that is to model the attitude we hope they will assume. If they see us being thankful, they will learn to be thankful.

–Tom McGrath, author of *Raising Faith-Filled Kids* (Loyola Press)

Bringing the Lesson Home

- Read with your child the pages that were sent home.

- Share a family thank-you meal. Take turns thanking each person for his or her special contribution to the family.

- Place the Grace at Meals prayer card by a different person each day, indicating whose turn it is to lead the meal prayer.

- Make a renewed effort to encourage all members of the family to use the words *please* and *thank you*.

- Before your family's Thanksgiving meal, let each person thank God for a blessing received.

- Make it a family habit to thank God daily for blessings received, perhaps at mealtime or bedtime.

CHAPTER 11

Preparing Is Good

God promised to send his Son, Jesus.
God's people waited and prayed.
God prepared to send Jesus.

At Christmas, we celebrate Jesus' birthday.
During Advent, we get ready for Christmas.
We light an Advent wreath.
Draw four candles on this Advent wreath.

We also make cookies and
other good things to eat.
Draw decorations on
each Christmas cookie.

Jesus' birthday is coming.
We prepare our hearts as gifts.
We will be loving to others.
We give Jesus the gift of our love.

Think about how you will show love
to your family and friends.
Draw a picture of it in the heart.
Pray, "Come, Lord Jesus."

Advent in Families

The Lesson Your Child Learned

Advent is the season of waiting and preparing to celebrate the threefold coming of Christ: his coming long ago as a man, his daily comings in grace through the sacraments and the events of our daily lives, and his future coming in glory. The children learned that Christmas commemorates the birth of God's Son, Jesus, who came for our salvation. Add "Come, Lord Jesus!" to your mealtime prayers.

Living the Lesson

Whenever someone utters the phrase, "He had his heart set on it," I think of young Ralphie Parker in the classic yuletide movie *A Christmas Story*. As Christmas approached, Ralphie absolutely ached to own the "Red Ryder, carbine-action, 200-shot, range model BB gun with a compass in the stock" that he saw on display at the local department store. Every time I see that film, I ache right along with Ralphie, because I can readily recall a number of Decembers I spent pining for a BB gun, a bike, or, when I was seven, a real pony.

If we're lucky, we never lose the habit of such Advent yearning; we simply change the object of our longing. Instead of the big-screen TV, diamond necklace, or holiday cruise that we "know" will finally satisfy us, we can learn to hope for a deeper experience with Jesus, the one who can truly make us whole, no matter what is under the tree.

Truth be told, aren't most of the things we set our hearts on bound to be disappointing if we don't have love at the center of our lives? That's the gift the Christ Child embodies—self-giving love for one and all. That's the gift to set your heart on through all the days of Advent. —Tom McGrath, author of *Raising Faith-Filled Kids* (Loyola Press)

Bringing the Lesson Home

- Read with your child the pages from this chapter that were sent home.

- In your family's celebration of the winter holidays, try to keep the season of Advent distinct from the Christmas season.

- Set up a stable without the figures of Jesus, Mary, and Joseph. Put the animals in the stable. Place the shepherds and sheep a short distance away.

- On Christmas Eve let everyone help place the figures of Jesus, Mary, and Joseph in the stable. Read aloud as a family the story of Jesus' birth from the Bible and sing "Silent Night."

CHAPTER 12

Choosing Is Good

We should think before we choose.

We want to make good choices.

When we make good choices,
we are happy.

God chose Mary to be the mother of Jesus.

Mary chose to do what God wanted.

Scripture

Mary said yes to God.

Based on Luke 1:38

Yes

Mary is the mother of Jesus.

Mary is our mother too.

Mary helps us say yes to God.

 Try This

Color and decorate the word Yes.

Color Mary's dress.

Ask Mary to help you say yes to God.

Choosing in Families

The Lesson Your Child Learned

Mary, the perfect follower of Jesus, shows us that we attain happiness and self-fulfillment by loving surrender in obedience to God's will. By their choices, family members contribute to family unity or take away from it. The self-control and good habits your child learns now lay the foundation for a moral life. In this chapter the children learned the importance of making good choices. They learned that Mary is their mother and will help them do what God wants.

Living the Lesson

Over the years I've come to recognize the small decisions that loom large in my life at home. Do I empty the dishwasher or leave it for someone else to do? Do I make an effort to call when I'm going to be late? Do I think to send a no-special-occasion card to my wife, parents, or daughters during the year to say, "You're special to me every day"? I see these seemingly small decisions as indicators of the healthiness of my commitments and relationships. If I'm withholding the small things, I know that in some way I'm also withholding my heart, which can have potentially large consequences.

The same is true with God. Do I make time for God at the beginning of the day? Do I thank him throughout the day for all the help that he sends my way? Do I look for the presence of God in others and treat them accordingly? If you focus on the small decisions that will open your heart, your relationships with your family and with God will reap giant rewards.

–Tom McGrath, author of *Raising Faith-Filled Kids* (Loyola Press)

Bringing the Lesson Home

- Read with your child the pages from this chapter that were sent home.

- Assist your child with the Hail Mary prayer printed on the back of the Mary card he or she brings home.

- Point out the happiness your child's good actions bring the family and the pain bad actions cause.

- Let your child make decisions and encourage him or her to stand by them.

- Guide your child to take responsibility for his or her actions. Be sure to model this behavior too.

- Let your child know what is acceptable behavior at home and in public and expect conformity. Take the time early on to explain the reasons for what you ask your child to do.

Celebrating the Church Year

There is a time for everything, and a time for every affair under the heavens.
A time to be born, and a time to die; a time to plant, and a time to uproot the plant.

Based on Ecclesiastes 3:1–2

To Everything There Is a Season

One of the many delights of having a child in kindergarten is that classroom lessons and activities revolve around the yearly calendar. Seasons and feast days, holidays and ordinary time make up a large part of the curriculum and, because the calendar is now a significant part of your child's life, it will become a noticeable part of yours. That is a very good thing, because living in harmony with the rhythms of the earth satisfies an ancient and universal, though often neglected, yearning: to feel part of the natural world around us.

The liturgical year of the Church mirrors and expands these natural rhythms. From the glowing candlelight on our Advent wreaths to the ashes that mark the beginning of Lent, to the abundance of flowers at a May Crowning, our seasonal symbols and liturgies seek to make visible that which is invisible: the loving presence of God in all things.

Making the Most of Time

We can make the most of the time we have, or let the moments of our life pass by. Here are some ways to add depth to the days you and your family spend together.

- Get each day off to a good start. Rather than getting caught up in a frantic rush, start the day with a simple prayer, offering God the "prayers, works, joys, and sufferings" of the day to come.

- Celebrate feasts and seasons. In addition to Christmas and Easter, make a point of celebrating a saint's day for each family member, either on the feast of the saint the person is named for or on the feast of his or her favorite saint. Get a calendar listing the main feast days of the church and make a point of celebrating in a special way at least once a month. Involve your child in preparing the festivities.

- Make ordinary moments special. During the long stretches of "ordinary time," plan a celebration or two, "just because." Have a special dessert at dinner or go out for ice cream "just because God made us a family."

- Create and appreciate family rituals. First, congratulate yourself on the positive family rituals your family has already adopted. You might also consider picking a night of the week as family night—a time for games, watching a movie, telling or reading aloud stories, riding bikes, or doing another fun activity as a family. Make it a time everyone can count on being together.

Making the Most of Time *continued*

- Savor the gift of the present moment. Jesus said, "The kingdom of God is among you." (Luke 17:21) Realize that this present moment is the one in which we can encounter God—not some distant and theoretical time in the future, but right here and right now. Be open to and look for evidence of God's presence in your life right now:

  a. in the joyful innocence of your child

  b. in the strength you receive to rise to the challenges you face during the day

  c. in the acts of loving kindness you receive from family members, neighbors, and even strangers

  d. in the beauty of nature, the joy of music, the creativity of artists, the goodness of people who sacrifice for others, and the sheer exuberance of being alive

- Attend the seasonal liturgical celebrations in your parish as often as possible. They are often family friendly, and they will help nurture in you and in your child a sense of the sacredness of each season throughout the year.

- Take regular walks with your child to look for signs of the season. Help sharpen your child's powers of observation by asking questions such as, "What is it that you like about what you see?"

The Practicing Catholic

Some years ago in the fall, I attended an exhibit of artists from Mexico. Each artist had created an *ofrenda,* or offering, to commemorate the life and times of a deceased family member. I was so moved by what I saw that I decided to make an *ofrenda* at home in memory of my father. I gathered photographs and a few other items that he had used and treasured during his life and placed them on the mantle in my living room. As I worked, long-forgotten incidents from my childhood came flooding back, and I remembered my father vividly in specific ways that I had not since he died—things like his twinkly eyes, his laugh, and especially the way his hands looked and felt. This ritual has become my treasured tradition on the Feast of All Souls, partly because of the powerful memories it evokes and partly because I can share them with my children.

Ann O'Connor, author of *The Twelve Unbreakable Principles of Parenting* (ACTA Publications)

Ofrenda for My Father, Ripot Garcia

Shepherds Are Good

A shepherd loves and cares for his sheep.

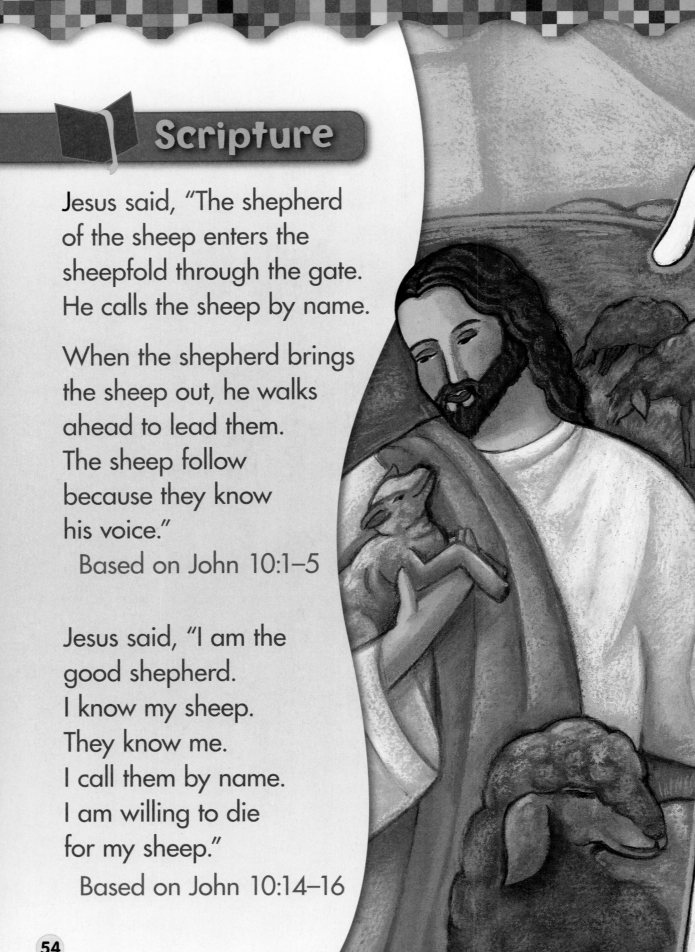

Jesus said, "The shepherd of the sheep enters the sheepfold through the gate. He calls the sheep by name.

When the shepherd brings the sheep out, he walks ahead to lead them. The sheep follow because they know his voice."

Based on John 10:1–5

Jesus said, "I am the good shepherd. I know my sheep. They know me. I call them by name. I am willing to die for my sheep."

Based on John 10:14–16

Jesus loves and cares for us.
We love Jesus, the
Good Shepherd.

Try This

Color the staff and the wolf.

Jesus, the Good Shepherd, knows
you and calls you by name.
What do you want to tell Jesus?

Shepherding in Families

The Lesson Your Child Learned

The relationship of love and trust that can exist between the human person and Christ is exemplified in the parable of the Good Shepherd. In this chapter the children learned about the protective love Jesus has for each of them as they heard the parable of the Good Shepherd. They received a Good Shepherd cutout set that they may set up at home as a reminder of Jesus' constant concern for them. We are all called to be shepherds in some way. Parents are responsible for their children's religious formation, teachers for the message they give the children.

Living the Lesson

You probably have many opportunities to serve as a good shepherd to people in your life, starting with the influence you have on the child in your care. It's important, then, that your interactions with these people aren't on autopilot. That is, you don't rush from activity to activity, from chore to chore, without stopping occasionally to be aware of where you are, who you are with, and what you are doing.

Here's a trick to help increase your awareness. The next time you and your child are doing something as simple as picking up toys and straightening things up in the family room, imagine yourself many years in the future looking back on this moment. From that vantage point, what seems important about this current moment? It probably isn't the orderliness of the family room as much as it is the time spent with this precious child at this time in his or her life.

Life in a family can be busy and demanding. It's also a time of miracles. Make it your spiritual goal to find ways to be mindful so that the busy-ness and the demands don't make you miss the miracles.

–Tom McGrath, author of *Raising Faith-Filled Kids* (Loyola Press)

Bringing the Lesson Home

- Read with your child the pages from this chapter that were sent home.

- Invite your child to say or to sing Psalm 23:1. Have your child use the Good Shepherd cutouts to tell the parable.

- Find age-appropriate ways to let your child show care for others.

Hearts Are Good

Love is a special gift God puts in our hearts.
Love is a special gift God puts in our hearts.
God's love makes us happy.
God sent Jesus into the world
to show us his love.

Jesus loves everyone.

Jesus wants us to love everyone too.

Jesus showed love for his friends.
We bring Jesus' love to others.

Scripture

Jesus says, "Love one another
as I love you."   Based on John 13:34

- Connect the dots from 1 to 10.
- See what Jesus gave his friends.
- Color it.
- Draw a fire on the sticks where Jesus cooked breakfast for his friends.

Thank God for the gift of love.

Loving in Families

The Lesson Your Child Learned

God's love was fully revealed to us in Jesus. The Christian religion is based on a love relationship between God and the human person. We want our children to realize that God loves them personally. They learn to accept themselves as persons worthy to be loved by God and by others. In this chapter the children heard again about God's great love for them as shown through Jesus and through the loving people God places in their lives. They were invited to share in Jesus' love by showing love for others. They heard about Jesus' love for his friends in the story of the large catch of fish and cooking breakfast. (John 21:1–14)

Living the Lesson

Think of all the books, movies, TV shows, songs, and soap operas that gain dramatic tension by observing two people on the verge of falling in love. They capture and convey a longing that seems universal, as if the whole world is holding its breath, waiting for love to erupt in their lives.

This great longing is holy. It's a manifestation of our desire to know and to experience God's love for us. God placed this desire to know, love, and serve him deep in our hearts. God also sent his Son, the embodiment of divine love, as the true response to our deepest longing.

As parents we are in a position to teach our children about love by simply loving them well. At our best, we model the love of God in our own love. When we tend to our children when they're sick, listen to them when they are troubled, share their joy during play, and nurture their bodies, minds, and souls, we are preparing them to live a life of love. They become ready to expect God's love and are more likely to see signs of it all around them.

–Tom McGrath, author of *Raising Faith-Filled Kids* (Loyola Press)

Daniel
Cela
Maren

Bringing the Lesson Home

- Read with your child the pages from this chapter that were sent home.

- Ask your child to tell you about the heart pendant he or she received as a reminder to love as Jesus did.

- Encourage your child's efforts to show love and care for others at home, in the neighborhood, and at school. Notice times your child acts with loving kindness and commend him or her. Be specific.

- In secret, say or do something today to make every member of your family feel loved and appreciated.

CHAPTER 15

Hands Are Good

Our helping hands are gifts of love. With them, we give to others.

We show the love that's in our hearts for our sisters and brothers.

Our hands can bring us blessings too, for they help us share our love.

Our loving deeds bring happiness and special joys from God above.

Scripture

Two men who were blind heard that Jesus was passing by.

They shouted, "Lord, have mercy on us!"

Jesus stopped and asked, "What do you want me to do for you?"

They said, "Lord, let us see."

He touched their eyes.

They could see.

The two men followed Jesus, praising God.

Based on
Matthew 20:30–34

Jesus helped people.
We will help people too.

I can use my hands to help others.

 # Try This

Circle the pictures that
show how you can help.

How do you feel when
you have helped others?

Thank God for the gift
of your helping hands.

Service in Families

The Lesson Your Child Learned

Jesus made it known through his words and actions that he came not to be served, but to serve. He taught self-giving as the way to human fulfillment. Children will find meaning in life through love of God and others if they live in families in which they witness generous self-giving service. In this chapter the children heard the story of Jesus helping two blind men by his healing touch. They learn that Jesus calls them to be helpers too.

Living the Lesson

My mother turned 80 recently, and it was time for a lot of reminiscing. One thing that all our memories shared in common is that in every story Mom was usually busy doing some kind of service for others. And upon further reflection, no matter how serious the cause, Mom and her friends always made sure they had fun. Even now, her calendar is peppered with volunteering at a hospital thrift store, leading religious education sessions with special-needs children, and just about any other need that surfaces at her local parish.

Now I see this same pattern woven into the lives of her children and grandchildren. Children learn a lot by osmosis, that is, by absorbing what's present in their environment. As parents it's easy to get caught up doing for our children. And that is necessary and good. But we also owe them the example of doing for others in a spirit of joyful generosity. Their little eyes are watching.

–Tom McGrath, author of *Raising Faith-Filled Kids* (Loyola Press)

Bringing the Lesson Home

- Read with your child the pages from this chapter that were sent home.

- Encourage your child to help others and acknowledge his or her contributions. Be specific.

- Let your child see your willingness to help those both inside and outside your family circle. Encourage your child to make such contributions as well.

- Adopt an elderly person in your neighborhood. Have your child make a card or gift for the person and/or visit him or her regularly.

- Find ways for your child to participate in daily household tasks.

CHAPTER 16

Forgiveness Is Good

It is not easy to always be loving.
Sometimes we do things
that do not please God.

Sometimes we hurt others.
This is a sin.
When we sin, we are not happy.

But we can say "I'm sorry."
Then we will be happy again.

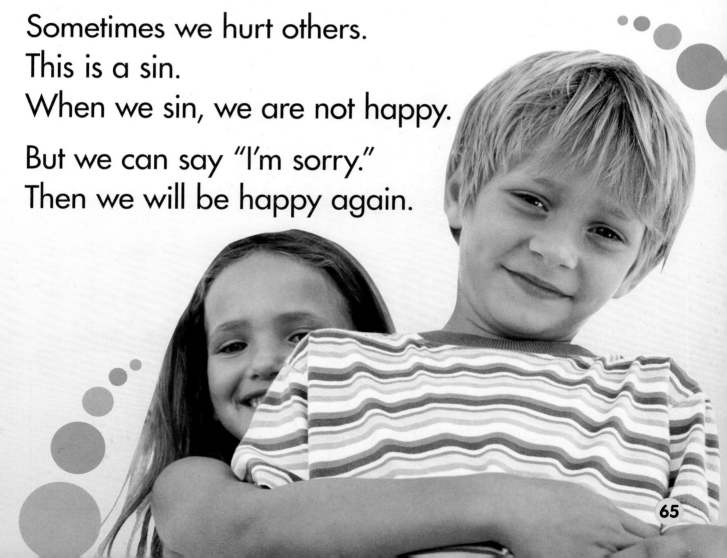

Jesus wants us to be loving.

When we hurt someone,
we say "I'm sorry."
Jesus forgives us when
we say "I'm sorry."

Then we show our love as God's children.
We forgive like Jesus.
We forgive those who hurt us.

Scripture

Jesus said, "Forgive others from your heart."

Based on Matthew 18:35

Jesus forgave Zacchaeus, a thief.

Find Zacchaeus in the tree. Circle him.

Trace over and color the words I'm Sorry.

Do you need to say "I'm sorry" to someone?

Forgiveness in Families

The Lesson Your Child Learned

Our ability to feel and to express emotions enriches our lives. In themselves, feelings are neither good nor bad. We all have a need to admit our feelings and to take responsibility for the way we express them. Children who live in families where forgiving and being forgiven are part of life easily learn to accept God's forgiveness. In this chapter, the children explored some of their feelings and were made aware of others' feelings. They learned that it is wrong to hurt themselves, to hurt others, or to damage property when angry. They learned how to say "I'm sorry" when they hurt someone's feelings, and they heard Jesus tell them to forgive those who hurt them.

Living the Lesson

Did you ever play the game "hot potato"? I remember both the joy and the fear we had as kids as we hurriedly passed the "hot potato" so we didn't end up with it and get eliminated from the game. Sometimes families treat feelings like hot potatoes. When an uncomfortable emotion arises, each person tries to pass along that charged feeling to someone else.

There are three steps families can take to short-circuit the hot potato game. One, become aware of your own emotional state. Two, ask for God's help in responding appropriately to the emotions you find the most troublesome. Three, respond rather than react. Responding means that you don't just pass along the emotional charge. Instead you might calmly say, "It sounds as though you are upset. Let's figure out what you're feeling." And if your child expresses his or her emotions in a way that goes against your values, use that as a teachable moment, saying, "We don't talk to one another like that. It's okay to have your feelings, but it's not okay to be mean."

–Tom McGrath, author of *Raising Faith-Filled Kids* (Loyola Press)

Bringing the Lesson Home

- Read with your child the pages from this chapter that were sent home.

- Make room in your family for one another's feelings. Do not encourage repressing feelings, but teach your child how to deal with the feelings that come up. Welcome the feelings and coach them about the behavior.

- Readily say "I'm sorry" when you have acted in ways that don't live up to your values of respect and care for others.

© LoyolaPress.

CHAPTER 17

Church Is Good

At our Baptism, we became members of the Catholic Church.

The Church is a family of people who believe in Jesus.

God's family, the Church, follows Jesus' way of love.

God's family gathers together to worship God our Father.

God's family gathers together to worship God in a special building. It is called a church.

Scripture

We are joyful in God's house of prayer.

Based on Isaiah 56:7

The priest leads the people who gather to pray. Together the priest and people are called the Church.

Jesus is present in the church building in a special way. Jesus is also present with his people, the Church.

I belong to _____ Church.

Try This

Draw a picture of something you saw in God's house.

Thank God that you belong to the Church.

The Church in Families

The Lesson Your Child Learned

Catholics first receive spiritual life at Baptism. This life is strengthened with Confirmation and nourished through the Eucharist. Throughout our lives, we grow in our understanding of what it really means to be incorporated into Jesus' passion, death, and Resurrection. It is through their parents' faith that children first learn what it is to be Catholic, witnessing to Jesus as members of his Church in the world today. In this chapter, the children heard again that they were made members of the Church through Baptism. They learned about the role of the priest and the other members of the parish community.

Living the Lesson

No matter what time of the day or night, somewhere around the world, people are gathering in Catholic churches to celebrate the Eucharist. Every day, in places all over the world, people are joining together as Christians to feed the hungry, heal the sick, tend to the brokenhearted, and preach the Good News.

What is the Church? It is as simple as a family saying their mealtime prayers together. It's as complex as the gathering of cardinals from all over the globe, representing every ethnic group and culture, deliberating on the great moral issues of the day. The Church is a group of believers who believe a common set of beliefs. It's a movement as well as a mission. The Church is the Body of Christ.

For most of us, when we hear the word *church*, we think about our local parish church because it is the place we gather to hear the Word of God and be fed by the Bread of Life. But remember that you are the Church too. You are called to bring the light of Christ wherever you go—even to your own home.   –Tom McGrath, author of *Raising Faith-Filled Kids* (Loyola Press)

Bringing the Lesson Home

- Read with your child the pages from this chapter that were sent home.

- Bring your child to Sunday Mass with you. Encourage your child to join in saying the Our Father and other Mass prayers.

- Use the Our Father as part of your family prayer.

CHAPTER 18

Meals Are Good

On the night before he died, Jesus ate a meal with the apostles. It was Jesus' last supper with them.

At this meal, Jesus gave thanks and praise to his Father. Jesus offered himself to his Father for us. Jesus gave himself to us as bread and wine.

As God's family, we come together at Mass. We give God thanks and praise.

We hear God's Word in the Bible.

We remember Jesus' Last Supper.

We remember that Jesus died for all of us. Jesus gives himself to us in the Eucharist.

At Mass the bread and wine become the Body and Blood of Jesus. Jesus gives us the gift of himself in Holy Communion.

Scripture

Jesus said, "Do this in memory of me."

Based on Luke 22:19

Try This

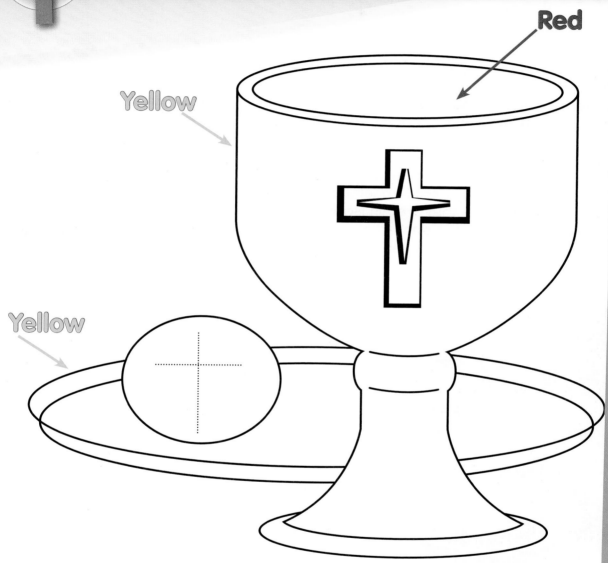

Red

Yellow

Yellow

Color the wine in the cup red.

Color the cup and the plate yellow.

Trace over the cross on the bread.

Sharing Meals in Families

The Lesson Your Child Learned

At the Last Supper Jesus gave us the everlasting gift of himself. He offered his life as a sacrifice to his Father. He gave himself as food to strengthen us, to unite himself with us, and to unite us with one another. The Mass, then, is both a sacrifice and a meal. In this chapter, the children learned that meals are times for sharing love as well as for sharing food. They heard the story of Jesus' Last Supper and learned that at Mass Jesus offers himself up for us and feeds us with the bread and wine that are his Body and Blood. Through the love and friendship shared at family meals, children experience the human values found in the Eucharist.

Living the Lesson

Do you want to strengthen your family? Eat meals together regularly. Recent studies have shown that children whose families eat together regularly get better grades, enjoy better nutrition, and have a lower incidence of drug use and other problematic behavior. They're also more likely to practice their faith.

When we come together at the kitchen table, we bring not only our physical hunger, but also our social, emotional, and spiritual hungers. At the family meal, all these hungers are fed. In a time when children are being tossed about on the stormy seas of life, the family meal provides an anchor within a safe harbor—the family.

The biggest benefit of the family meal is that it prepares us all to come to the table of the Lord in the Eucharist. The more we can be present to one another at our own kitchen table, the more we will be able to experience the Real Presence of Jesus in the Eucharist.

–Tom McGrath, author of *Raising Faith-Filled Kids* (Loyola Press)

Bringing the Lesson Home

- Read with your child the pages from this chapter that were sent home.

- Discuss the day's activities as a family at mealtime.

- Have a family baking project and enjoy the results at your family meal.

- Give your child the job of setting the table.

- Begin each family meal with a prayer. Let your child lead the prayer from time to time.

To Forgive and to Serve

Forgiveness in the Family

The movie *Home Alone* may remain so popular because it shows what happens when a mom and her young son are not behaving at their best. This is not an unusual situation in families, so we can all relate to this family's dilemma. Tension in the household is running high, and Kevin McAllister and his mom say things they both end up regretting. The golden moment of the film is when mother and son are reunited by sharing the simple words, "I'm sorry." Some of the very best moments in a family come when forgiveness is freely offered and received all around.

The *Catechism of the Catholic Church* says, "[T]he home is the first school of Christian life...." It is the place where we "learn endurance and the joy of work, fraternal love, [and] generous—even repeated—forgiveness...." (*CCC #1657*) As fallible human beings, we need to learn to forgive as well as how to ask to be forgiven. What a blessing it is to live in a home where forgiveness is generously given and received. Forgiveness is a hallmark of Christian life.

When we recite the Our Father, the prayer Jesus taught us, we say, "Forgive us our trespasses as we forgive those who trespass against us." In that short passage, Jesus described forgiveness as an essential part of Christian life. Forgiveness is like a river; its nature is to flow and we know that it flows first and foremost from the heart of God. Because we are forgiven, we are able to forgive others.

One of the most important faith lessons you can teach your child is how to say, "I'm sorry" and "I forgive you." That's because God's love for us comes wrapped in forgiveness. The more we can accept forgiveness and pass it on to others, the more capacity we will have to receive and give God's love.

Children learn best from what's modeled to them. In homes where the words "I'm sorry" and "I forgive you" are heard frequently in the course of family life, children develop the confidence to expect forgiveness and the hope that reconciliation will be the result.

Getting Started

Some lessons are best learned by practice. Here are a few suggestions on how you can make your home a school of Christian life by modeling the virtue of forgiveness.

- When your child has done something you need to correct, ask in an unshaming way, "Do you understand what you did wrong?" or "Do you understand how your behavior hurt your sister?" The point is not punishment as much as it is helping your child grow in awareness.

- When correcting your child, be sure to make a distinction between the behavior and the person. For example, say, "Hitting other people is wrong because it will hurt them." instead of "You're a bad boy for hitting Jason." This is not to let the child "off the hook" but will help him or her, over time, build empathy and understand the consequences of his or her actions.

- When you've acted in a way you regret, model for your child the way to ask forgiveness:

  1. Say you are sorry.

  2. Be specific as to what you are sorry for.

  3. Make an honest promise to do better in the future. This might sound something like this: "Jennifer, I'm sorry that I yelled at you in the car. I was worried I was going to be late, and I didn't take time to listen to your questions. I hope you'll forgive me. I will try to leave more time between errands next time so that I'll have time to listen to your questions."

- Let your child see you give and receive forgiveness with other family members. Apologizing is not a sign of weakness. It is an acknowledgement that we adults can fail, and that forgiveness is important to us too.

- The next time you pray the Our Father as a family, point out to your child the phrase, "Forgive us our trespasses as we forgive those who trespass against us." Explain that Jesus wants us to forgive one another and to ask for forgiveness when we haven't been loving to one another. Forgiveness is a sign that God is in our home.

- Tell your child the story of the Good Shepherd who seeks out the lost sheep. (Luke 15:3–7) This is a good opportunity to let your child know that Jesus is always ready to forgive us no matter what we do. We just need to tell him we're sorry.

Seeds Are Good

Put a seed into the ground
To die so a plant can grow.
With sun and water from God,
New life sprouts and starts to show.
Apple seeds make apple trees,
Potato seeds, potatoes.

Radish seeds grow radishes,
Tomato seeds, tomatoes.
Flower seeds grow marigolds,
Violets, and roses, too.
Each seed that dies and grows
Tells God's love for me and you.

A seed dies to give a plant new life. Jesus died to give us new life so that we can live in love as Jesus did.

Jesus gave his life for us!

Scripture

Jesus said, "Unless a grain of wheat falls to the ground and dies, it remains just a grain of wheat; but if it dies, it produces much fruit."

Based on John 12:24

A cross is a sign of Jesus' love for us.

When we make the Sign of the Cross, we show we love God.

Try This

Connect the dots to make a cross.

Color the heart.

When you make the Sign of the Cross, remember Jesus' love.

The Cross in Families

The Lesson Your Child Learned

The children were introduced to the mystery of life and death through a poem about a seed that dies to give new life to a plant. They learned that through Jesus' cross, they received new life in Baptism to enable them to live in love as Jesus did. Find a good place for the cross your child brought home to use when saying daily prayers.

Living the Lesson

In his wonderful book *The Sign of the Cross* (Loyola Press), Bert Ghezzi recounts the story of when author Alexander Solzhenitsyn was exiled to a Soviet prison camp. After months of hard labor, little food, and crushing cold, Solzhenitsyn left the line of workers and sat down. He knew that soon a guard would come and command him back to work. If he refused, it would mean a swift death, yet that seemed preferable to continuing.

Before a guard could intervene, an old prisoner came and knelt before Solzhenitsyn and with a stick, scratched out the shape of a cross in the dirt. Ghezzi writes, "Solzhenitsyn looked at the cross, and as he reflected on it, a ray of light penetrated his dark thoughts. In that moment his perspective changed radically. He realized that he did not have to face the evil of the gulag and the Soviets on his own diminished strength. With the power of the cross, he could withstand the evil of not one but a thousand Soviet empires."

In our Baptism, we have been united with Christ's death and Resurrection. Through the cross, Jesus freed us from slavery to sin and death and became the source of eternal life. We are called to take up our cross in the dyings and risings that are part of our everyday life.

–Tom McGrath, author of *Raising Faith-Filled Kids* (Loyola Press)

Bringing the Lesson Home

- Read with your child the pages from this chapter that were sent home.

- Let your child plant some seeds in a pot or make a small garden. Talk about the way a seed dies to give life to a plant.

- Teach your child how to make the Sign of the Cross.

- Encourage your child to make the Sign of the Cross with holy water when entering a church. When we do this, we recall our Baptism.

CHAPTER 20

Butterflies Are Good

A butterfly gives us joy. It has new life.
On Easter, Jesus rose from
the dead with new life.
We celebrate his new life with great joy.
We sing ALLELUIA!

Scripture

"You are looking for Jesus.
He has been raised."
Based on Mark 16:6

83

Jesus rose to new life.
We can share the good news.
We can live Jesus' new life.

We can show love for God and others.
How will you show love?

In springtime, signs of new life
are everywhere.
They tell us to live Jesus' life of love.
Butterflies remind us of Jesus' new life.

Try This

Find the 11 hidden butterflies.
Circle them.
Praise God that Jesus is risen.
Pray the Easter word Alleluia.

New Life in Families

The Lesson Your Child Learned

Jesus is risen. His victory over sin and death is our triumph as well. We are assured that our yearnings for wholeness and fullness of life will be fulfilled. Although we experience suffering, we believe the power of the Resurrection will transform our pain into new life and glory, and we believe our lives are transformed even now. In this chapter, the children were led to wonder and delight in the various forms of new life evident in the spring. They compared the life cycle of a butterfly to Jesus' death and Resurrection, and they heard that through Baptism, they participated in Jesus' new life and can live his life of love.

Living the Lesson

Each day as I walked to the train, I saw a dandelion pushing its way up through a crack in the sidewalk. Others may have seen it as a blight on the landscape, but I took it as a sign of hope.

The dandelion was growing right outside an abandoned warehouse. The warehouse used to be bustling with activity, but now it stood silent. It was a difficult time in my own life, a time when I felt stymied and uncertain about my own future. And yet here, bursting forth from the smallest crack in the concrete, was a bright yellow dandelion, defying all odds. Somehow that spunky little plant was the symbol of courage and perseverance I needed.

New life springs up all around us—in our gardens, in our children, in our neighborhoods, and in ourselves. God continually offers you the gift of new life. Open your heart to it today.

–Tom McGrath, author of *Raising Faith-Filled Kids* (Loyola Press)

Bringing the Lesson Home

- Read with your child the pages from this chapter that were sent home.

- Go for a walk and look for signs of new life.

- Visit a church to see the baptismal font where your new life and/or your child's new life began.

- Teach your child to identify some spring flowers. Look for robins. Tell why they are signs of spring.

- Bring new life into your home by buying a small plant or by letting your child pick spring flowers and put them in a vase.

- Read aloud Mark's account of the Resurrection, 16:1–7. Let your child sense your joy in the Easter event and in Jesus' being alive and with us today.

CHAPTER 21

Light Is Good

God knows we need light.

He gives us the gift of the sun.

Jesus is a light for us too.

Jesus helps us see how to love God by loving others.

Scripture

Jesus said, "I am the light of the world." Based on John 8:12

Our hearts are bright with Jesus' love.

Jesus wants his love to shine through us. We light up the world with Jesus' love.

We show love for God and others.

We let the light
of Jesus' love shine
through us.

Try This

Make the light
shine through
the darkness.
Color the rays
bright colors.

How will you
share the light
of Jesus' love?

Light in Families

The Lesson Your Child Learned

In this chapter the children were led to appreciate light as a gift of God. They heard Jesus call himself the light of the world and learned that the Easter candle is a symbol of the risen Jesus. The children were told about the candle they received at Baptism to show that they share in Jesus' life. They took home candles that they made as reminders to let their light shine by being loving to their families.

Living the Lesson

When you were young, did you sing the song "This little light of mine, I'm gonna let it shine"? You might sing it now with your child. The message is a good one, and one you can practice every day.

Jesus said to his first followers, "You are the light of the world." He said we shouldn't hide our light, but instead we should let it shine before all. To be the light of the world, the source of your illumination must be God. The closer you allow yourself to be to God, the more his light will shine through you for the good of all.

Sometimes we hide our light under the bushel basket of preoccupations, worries, insecurities, impatience, or other temporary moods. Think of how you greet your family members each day. Does your light shine on them? Or is it hidden beneath your daily concerns and cares? Pray today that God will help you let your light shine to warm your family and to help them grow in the reflected glow of God's love.

–Tom McGrath, author of *Raising Faith-Filled Kids* (Loyola Press)

Bringing the Lesson Home

- Read with your child the pages from this chapter that were sent home.

- The next time you are together in church, point out the tall Easter candle. It is a symbol of Jesus, risen and alive.

- Make or buy a family candle as a reminder that Jesus is the light of the world and is present in the midst of your family. Take turns lighting the candle before family prayers. Younger children can blow it out.

- Enjoy stargazing with your child. Watch a sunrise or sunset together.

- Talk about ways you can conserve electricity in order to share God's gift of light with others.

CHAPTER 22

Celebrating Is Good

Gifts are a sign of love.

We thank people for gifts.

God's gifts are signs of his great love. We give thanks for God's gifts at Mass.

We celebrate God's love.

Scripture

They devoted themselves to the breaking of the bread and to the prayers.

Based on Acts of the Apostles 2:42

Sunday is the Christian day of celebration.
We celebrate with God's family at Mass.

A priest leads the celebration.

We hear God's Word.

We sing and pray and give gifts.

We remember that Jesus died and rose to new life.

We thank Jesus for his great love.

God wants us to celebrate his love and goodness at Sunday Mass.

 **Try This**

Draw an altar for the priest celebrating Mass.

Draw a candle on each end. Draw a cross in the center.

Thank God for inviting you to Mass.

Celebrating in Families

The Lesson Your Child Learned

Studies show that children are profoundly affected by early religious experiences. Habits of prayer are best learned by praying with others and joining in the celebration of the Mass. In this chapter the children discovered the meaning of gifts and were shown how to thank God at Mass for the gifts of his love. The children learned that they are invited, by reason of their Baptism, to join in the Sunday Mass celebration.

Living the Lesson

And the band sang, "Celebrate good times, come on!" We were at a family wedding, and everyone was on the dance floor. Old and young, limber and lame, great dancers and klutzes, we all joined the dance and everyone belonged. My wife and I were dancing with our young daughters, but we knew we were really dancing with the whole extended family, and it felt like we were dancing with every person in the world. In that moment I sensed the oneness that Jesus prayed we might all achieve.

Celebrating is a deeply human trait. Unlike God's other earthly creatures, people celebrate birthdays and weddings, anniversaries and achievements. In doing so, we grow in awareness that all good gifts—love, fidelity, longevity, and life itself—come from God. Make sure to celebrate family events both large and small. Be aware of the One who makes it all possible.

–Tom McGrath, author of *Raising Faith-Filled Kids* (Loyola Press)

Bringing the Lesson Home

- Read with your child the pages from this chapter that were sent home.

- Use the Mass cutouts your child brought home.

- Take your kindergartner to church to celebrate Sunday Mass. Continue with a special meal or activity that shows Sunday is special.

- Let your child see that singing, praying, and receiving Holy Communion at Mass are important to you.

- Go through a family photo album and look at pictures of family celebrations, such as weddings, Baptisms, and reunions. Tell stories about how you celebrated these events.

CHAPTER 23

Air Is Good

God gives us the gift of air.

We cannot see air.

We can see what moving air does.

We need air to live.

Jesus gives us the gift of the Holy Spirit.

We cannot see the Holy Spirit.

The Holy Spirit fills us with love.

We can see what love does.

We need the Holy Spirit to love as Jesus does.

Scripture

Jairus's little girl was very sick. He asked Jesus for help. Jesus went with Jairus to his house. Before they got there, the little girl died. Jesus entered the house. He brought the little girl back to life.

Based on Luke 8:40–56

Jesus is with us always.
He is with us in his spirit of love.

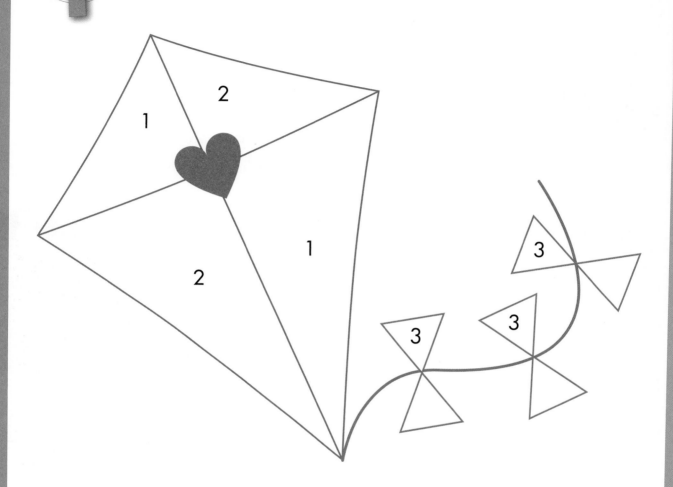

Draw swirls to show the wind around the kite.

Color the kite this way:
1. ▬▬▬▬
2. ▬▬▬▬
3. ▬▬▬▬

As you color, think of loving things you did this week.

The Spirit at Work in Families

The Lesson Your Child Learned

In this chapter, after learning about air (wind), an invisible reality that is necessary for life, the children were introduced to the invisible reality of the Holy Spirit, whose help we need to live as Christians. The Holy Spirit invites us to live Jesus' loving response to God, to love others, and to show responsible stewardship for the earth.

Living the Lesson

Some of the best advice I've ever gotten was from a mentor who, when I'd call on him with some frantic question, would say, "First, take a few deep breaths." I've used that advice during difficult moments at work, at home, and even before I get up to serve as lector at my parish on Sundays. Breathe. Simply breathe.

Being aware of your breathing is a great tool for getting out of worry and into the present moment. There's nothing more immediate and essential to life than inhaling and exhaling. Consciousness of your breathing can be a helpful prayer practice as well. It's a way to be present in the now and open to the God who dwells within us.

How close to us is God? In the second account of the creation of human beings (Genesis 2:7), God breathed into Adam's nostrils the breath of life. God didn't just breathe air into the man; God breathed divine life into him. The Holy Spirit flows through us each moment of our lives. The more we realize just how close God chooses to be to us, the easier it will be to live accordingly.

–Tom McGrath, author of *Raising Faith-Filled Kids* (Loyola Press)

Bringing the Lesson Home

- Read with your child the pages from this chapter that were sent home.

- Teach your child to be open the inspirations of the Holy Spirit by setting aside time each day for your child to pray. When your child begins to make more and more decisions, encourage him or her to pray for guidance. The most powerful way to teach this is to model it yourself.

- Reflect on whether or not your actions indicate that you prize people more than things. Examine how dependent you are on money and material things for happiness. Ask whether you use money to develop yourself as a person or to acquire more possessions.

- Encourage your child's growth in wonder by providing opportunities for silence, discovery, sharing, and surprise.

- Engage in healthy, fresh-air recreation.

CHAPTER 24

Joy Is Good

Jesus brought joy to the world.

He wants us to share his joy.

Loving and helping others brings them joy.

It brings us joy too.

Look at the pictures above.

Who is giving joy to others?
Who needs joy?
How would you bring
joy to them?

Christians bring joy
to others.
**We show that we
love God.**

Scripture

Jesus said, "I have told you how to love others so that my own joy may be in you, and your joy may be complete."

Based on John 15:11

Try This

Draw a line from each joy balloon to a person receiving joy.

Color the balloons. Ask God to help you bring joy to others.

Joy in Families

The Lesson Your Child Learned

Christians have every reason to rejoice. Through his glorious Resurrection, Jesus has assured us that we can live in endless joy. In this chapter the children learned that the risen Jesus is the source of Christian joy and that they are called to be joy-bringers. They were encouraged to go beyond self-centeredness, to reach out to others in self-sacrificing love, and to bring joy to those whom they meet.

Living the Lesson

When I think of the word *joy*, I think of my elderly neighbor walking hand in hand toward the park with his three-year-old granddaughter. As they toddle along together, she is wonder-struck by all she sees, and my neighbor beams with the sheer joy of her presence in his life.

Before her arrival in the world, he was a gruff guy, a hard-nosed sales manager who barked orders at those around him. Now we see the softer side of our neighbor. He has joy in his life, and it has transformed him.

Joy can transform us too. The world encourages us to grasp at pleasure. But joy arrives not as something to be pursued but as a gift to be received with gladness. All we need to do is make room for joy. Sometimes that takes the form of slowing our hectic pace and leaning down to hold the hand of innocence. Tonight, spend a few moments silently watching your child sleep as you let joy seep into your life.

–Tom McGrath, author of *Raising Faith-Filled Kids* (Loyola Press)

Bringing the Lesson Home

- Read with your child the pages from this chapter that were sent home.

- Help your child realize that disappointments and hardships are part of everyone's life and can take away our deep inner joy only if we let them.

- Do something this week as a family to bring joy to someone outside your immediate family.

- Tell your child that seeing him or her happy gives you joy and pleases Jesus. Being happy is one way of spreading Jesus' joy.

- Let your child be a child. Too often parents and guardians rush their children to take on activities and ways of dressing that are beyond their years. Letting your child enjoy childhood provides a solid foundation for a more joyful life in years to come.

CHAPTER 25

Life Is Good

Jesus gave us a life that will never end.

We have this life now.

We will have it forever in heaven.

Jesus lives in heaven with the Father and the Holy Spirit.

Jesus lives in us too.

Scripture

Jesus said, "I came so that they might have life."

Based on John 10:10

One day Jesus will come in glory.

He will gather us together in his kingdom.

There will be no more sadness.

We will be together with God and Mary, the saints, and all our loved ones.

In heaven we will be happy forever because we love God.

Life and Death in Families

The Lesson Your Child Learned

The greatest gift God has given is the precious gift of life. Yet it is only in dying that we are born to eternal life. Life reaches its fullness in heaven. In this chapter the children recalled that new life comes through death. The children learned that the greatest joy of heaven will be experiencing God's overwhelming love. In heaven, they will also enjoy the company of the blessed—including family and other loved ones who have died in faith.

Living the Lesson

I can hear it now: my dad taking a deep breath and saying, "Ahh, now *this* is really living." He'd say it when we stood fishing on his summer-house pier shortly after dawn, when we walked along the golf-course fairway on a crisp fall day, or right before we said grace before a holiday meal with the whole family gathered together.

The lesson we learned from his frequent pronouncement that "this is really living" is that life is meant to be savored. I think my father had an especially keen appreciation for life because of his job. He worked for 42 years at a Catholic cemetery, and he compassionately stood by those who mourned every working day of his life. He knew the preciousness and meaning that the reality of death adds to life. He also believed deeply that for those who have passed on in faith, life has not ended, only changed.

What, for you, constitutes "really living"? What can you do in your own life and in the life of your family to cultivate a deeper appreciation of the gift of life? Make time to savor the gift of life.

–Tom McGrath, author of *Raising Faith-Filled Kids* (Loyola Press)

Bringing the Lesson Home

- Read with your child the pages from this chapter that were sent home.

- In the way you treat other people, animals, and plants, teach your child to show reverence for life in all its forms.

- Visit grandparents and other elderly family members.

- Express joy at the birth of babies among relatives and friends.

- When someone you care about dies, explain that you grieve because you miss the loved one, but you know the person has a new life with God.

- As a family, pray for those who have died.

"For where two or three are gathered together in my name, there am I in the midst of them."

Matthew 18:20

Families at Mass

"Do This in Memory of Me."

Memory is a remarkable human trait. In basic biology we learned that all the cells in our bodies are continually being replaced, and that we are physically not the same person we were a few years ago. Yet somehow—amazingly—memory is passed along from one cell to another. We are able to remember who we are, what happened last year, and exactly how we like our eggs. Memory is nothing less than a divine tool, a gift from God that allows us to function on a daily basis. It is also the way we bring people and experiences from the past into the present moment.

Memory has a dual nature. It is like fire—with careful tending it can provide warmth and light, but if left unattended it will consume everything in its path. Likewise, we can use our memory to practice the art of reflection, or we can use it to avoid living in the present by wallowing in the past.

Mass is a re-creation of a memory. When we gather in church each week, we use our memory for its highest purpose: to recall the words and deeds of Jesus, to remember that we are his followers, and to decide what we must do to "love and serve the Lord."

Make the Most of the Mass

Here are ways you and your family members can get more meaning from your experience of the Mass.

- If Mass has become stale for you, try imagining that you are there for the first time. What do you notice that you haven't before? Try to see the beauty and the flow of the prayers and singing, reading and reflecting, and the sharing of the Body and Blood of Christ. It is there.

- Listen at each Mass for a particular word or phrase that speaks to you. Take it into your heart and reflect on it in your prayer times during the week.

- What does the sharing of the Body and Blood of Christ mean to you? Ask the members of your family who are old enough to answer this question at the dinner table.

- Make sure to have your child dip his or her fingers in the holy water on the way into church. Remind your child of his or her Baptism.

- Stop after Mass to light a vigil candle and to say a prayer for someone who has died or is ill. Ask whom your child would like to pray for.

- Have your child invite along friends, or include members of your extended family at Mass.

- Sing a favorite hymn as your grace before meals or while riding together in the car.

Make the Most of the Mass *continued*

- Give your child a short tour of your church. Try to convey a sense of the sacredness of the space. Notice any seasonal decorations and talk about why they are there. Look at a few stained-glass windows and see if you can tell what or whom they portray. Point out the lit candle next to the tabernacle that indicates the presence of the Blessed Sacrament. On your way out, draw your child's attention to the holy-water fonts at the doors and talk about why they are there.

A Practicing Catholic

Like many Catholics, I stopped going to Mass as soon as I began living on my own. But after my first child was born, I decided to give it another try. As I sat there week after week, a passage from 1 Corinthians came to mind; the one that begins "when I was a child, I used to talk as a child, think as a child, reason as a child. When I became a man, I put aside childish things." (13:11) It dawned on me that my view of the Mass had remained unchanged since high school. I had never stopped to think that as an adult and a parent, the prayers and readings might touch me in a different way. From that point on, I became more interested in what was happening. Then one Sunday I was sitting in the pew listening to the opening prayer when I felt an overwhelming wave of emotion run through my whole body. It was as though I was hearing the words for the first time and yet it was all so familiar, I started crying and couldn't stop. That was sixteen years ago. I've stopped crying since then, but I haven't stopped coming to Mass.

–Ann O'Connor, author of *The Twelve Unbreakable Principles of Parenting* (ACTA Publications)

Mass and Your Family

Families can face a variety of hurdles on the way to Mass each week—a stalling, whining child, our own fatigue, or ordinary inertia. But like all the other obstacles we overcome to ensure our child's well-being, getting to Mass is worth the effort we put into it. Nothing is as important to our child's spiritual welfare as being part of a faith community. The rhythm it establishes for the week, the hour of (relative) quiet, and simply being in the presence of a group of people while they sing, pray, reflect, ask forgiveness, and share the Body and Blood of Christ all have a powerful impact on a child. This is true even if it seems (and he or she claims) that your child is getting nothing out of the experience. It's just one more thing your child might not appreciate until he or she is grown up. Keep at it. You're giving your child a gift that can last an eternity.

Special Seasons and Days

Special Seasons

The seasons of spring, summer, fall, and winter are marked on the calendar. The Church also keeps a calendar of special seasons and days. The Church year includes the seasons of Advent, Christmas, Lent, Easter, and Ordinary Time. We celebrate God's love for us throughout the Church year.

Special Days

We like to celebrate special days. We celebrate special days during the Church year. We remember holy people who show us how to love God and follow Jesus.

The Year in Our Church

All Saints Are Good

People living in heaven with God are called saints. November 1 is the Feast of All Saints.

On this day we honor all the saints. We ask the saints to pray for us.

Saint Clare of Assisi, Saint Martin de Porres, and Saint Helen

Try This

We are all called to be saints. Draw a picture of yourself.

Ask your favorite saint to pray for you.

Halloween in Families

Halloween Blends the Holy and the Horrifying

Each year Halloween seems to receive more attention in our culture. It's a billion-dollar-a-year industry involving decorations, candy, costumes, and fun and scary activities for people of all ages. The holiday is rich in history and meaning, much of it religious, making it a great opportunity to combine fun with teaching our children about values.

A Quick History

Halloween as we know it today is a mixture of pagan, Christian, civic, and cultural influences. Various cultures have associated the day with witches, ghosts, and goblins. Many people trace its roots to an old Celtic festival, when the Celts believed the veil between the living and the dead was particularly thin. It was thought that on this night, the souls of those who had died could cross over into our mortal world. When Christian missionaries won over the hearts of the Celts, the popular feast was moved from spring to fall and celebrated as the feast of the eve of All Saints Day. Halloween comes from the word *hallowed* meaning "blessed" or "holy." So Halloween is the night where we eagerly anticipate the celebration of our living connection with the saints—all the faithful who have lived and died before us. It is fitting, then, that on the night before All Saints Day, our families remember and celebrate in a special way our belief in the Communion (close connection) of Saints.

Celebrating Your Values on Halloween

- Help your child research the saint he or she is named after or his or her favorite saint. Encourage your child to dress up as that favorite saint for Halloween.

- Tell your child that celebrating Halloween is a festive way to kick off the celebration of All Saints Day. We ask the saints to pray for us and to help us be good.

- At breakfast, recite a short litany of the family members who have died and whom you remember in your prayers. After each name, have everyone say, "Pray for us."

- Have fun! Make a special meal for dinner. Here's a quick idea for a healthy meal to offset the abundance of candy. Give each family member a paper plate. Put out bowls of olives, cucumbers, radishes, raisins, dried apricots or cranberries, cheese sticks, and cold cuts. Then have everyone make faces on his or her plate with the food. You can make scary faces or funny faces or both. Then everyone gets to eat what he or she created.

Advent Is Good

During Advent, God's family prepares to celebrate Jesus' birthday.

We light the Advent wreath. We pray, "Come, Lord Jesus."

 Try This

Color the candles and the Advent wreath.

Count the number of Sundays until Christmas.

Advent and Christmas in Families

Advent Helps Prepare Our Hearts

Sometimes the demands of preparing for Christmas can be such that we miss out on the joy of the season. This is a special year to observe and enjoy your child because he or she is beginning to learn more about the story of Jesus and the reason why we celebrate this special time. So set aside a night for family togetherness.

Celebrating Your Values at Christmastime

After a simple meal, bring out some favorite snacks and gather near the Christmas tree. Turn off all the lights in the room except the lights on the Christmas tree. Get comfortable and cozy. Here are some ideas to spur conversation and togetherness:

1. Take turns naming your favorite Christmas song and then sing it as a solo or all together. If you enjoyed it, sing it again.

2. Each person points to a favorite ornament on the tree and tells why he or she likes it. Maybe there's a special story about how it came to be on your tree.

3. Tell your child about a favorite Christmas memory from your childhood. Be sure to tell lots of details about how it felt when you were that age. Share any special lessons you learned "back in the olden days" of your youth.

4. Read aloud to the family. Pick a seasonal favorite such as Clement Moore's "'Twas the Night Before Christmas", Charles Dickens's *A Christmas Carol*, or the picture book *Who's That Knocking on Christmas Eve?* by Jan Brett.

5. Finish the reading with the following section from the Gospel of Luke 2:1–20, which tells about the birth of Jesus in Bethlehem.

Christmas Is Good

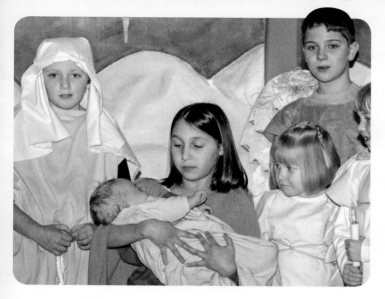

Christmas is Jesus' birthday. God our Father sent Jesus to us on the first Christmas.

Jesus came to show us how to love God.

Try This

Draw baby Jesus in the manger.

Thank God for sending us Jesus.

The Wise Men Are Good

The Wise Men went to see Jesus.

They gave Jesus gifts.

✝ Try This

Connect the dots to make the star.

Offer Jesus the gift of your love.

Lent Is Good

Lent is like springtime.

It is a time for us to grow. During Lent, we grow in God's love. We pray and do good deeds.

By Easter our hearts should be full of love.

 ## Try This

Color the leaves.

Each time you pray or do a good deed, color one flower petal.

> *Yet even now, says the* LORD, *return to me with your whole heart.* **Joel 2:12**

Lent in Families

Lent Offers Three Ways to Grow Spiritually

Parents are busy people, and busy people usually don't like disruptions. We've got our plans made and our schedules set. Then comes Lent. Lent is a season of interruptions, a disturber of complacency. It begins with Ash Wednesday, a day in which we bear upon our foreheads a sign that something different is happening to us. And it goes on for 40 days—a symbolic time echoing Moses' 40 years in the desert and Jesus' 40 days of preparation before beginning his public ministry. In Lent we take up practices that purposely disrupt our lives. We fast rather than feast. We add more prayer to our day. And we give to others rather than gather for ourselves.

Lent is a time to return to God with our whole heart. It's important to introduce your child to appropriate Lenten practices so that he or she will know the spiritual benefits of these sacred days of the Church year.

Celebrating Your Values During Lent

Fasting: We fast so that we might come to know a deeper hunger, our hunger and thirst for God. If we are always satisfied, we will not be moved to seek the one who truly satisfies our deepest longings. There are many ways to fast. We can

- fast one evening a week from television and video games. Play board games, read uplifting books, or tell stories to your child about the spiritual heroes from your own childhood.

- fast from criticizing family members, classmates, and coworkers. Find only good things to say about others, or hold your tongue.

Praying: Once we awaken our spiritual hunger, we can nurture it by spending more time in prayer. Here are some ways your family can add prayer to their day:

- Begin each morning with prayer together, offering God all your "prayers, works, joys, and sufferings of this day."

- Teach your child to pray while washing his or her hands. Point out that the water, like God's grace, pours freely to help cleanse us and refresh us.

Almsgiving: As we grow in awareness of our reliance on God, we are moved to generosity toward others.

- With your child, go through your closets and toy bins, and bring unwanted goods to the Saint Vincent De Paul Society or Goodwill.

- Give of your time together to visit a sick relative, neighbor, or fellow parishioner. Your child can brighten the day of someone who is homebound.

- Have your child help you prepare a bag of non-perishable food and household supplies for a local food pantry or shelter.

118

© LOYOLAPRESS.

Easter Is Good

On Easter morning, Jesus' disciples were surprised. They saw that the stone had been rolled away from the tomb.
Jesus' tomb was empty.
Jesus is alive! On Easter we pray Alleluia!

Try This

Put in order the events of the Easter story.

Holy Week and Easter in Families

Enter Into the Sacred Mysteries

Holy Week is the time each year when we enter into the sacred mysteries of Jesus' suffering, death, and Resurrection. The Church gathers to face the deepest questions that we have as human beings and to open our hearts to the lessons from the life and the example of Jesus. The events we observe this week are at the very heart of our faith and are the foundation on which we can build a life of faith for our families and ourselves.

Celebrating Your Values During Holy Week and Easter

The rituals and the retellings of the stories of our salvation are powerful. Participate in the Holy Week rites at your parish, and they will open up for you a sense of how these same sacred mysteries play out in our lives at home with our families.

Washing of the Feet: A lot of what parents teach is conveyed by example. Jesus followed this model, too, when he surprised his disciples by getting down on his knees and washing their feet. Think of the ways you serve your family by tending to their physical needs in feeding them, clothing them, and caring for them.

At the Last Supper, which we celebrate on Holy Thursday, Jesus used the sharing of the bread and wine to make real his continuing presence with us and for us in the Eucharist. Think of all the meals you share with your family and how you can make

them a source of real presence to one another and a point of awareness of God's presence in your home.

The Agony in the Garden: Jesus agonized over the consequences he knew would come from his faithfulness to the Father's will. Think of the times you struggle with standing firm on doing what you know is best for your family. Know that you are not alone.

Jesus Is Put to Death: Life in a family teaches us that there are many moments of dying to ourselves when we choose to respect, honor, and serve the needs of others and not just our own.

Jesus Is Raised to New Life: The reward for being faithful is new and abundant life, and we experience that in families too, when we experience forgiveness, connection, joy, and hope.

Pentecost Is Good

Jesus promised that he would send the Holy Spirit. On Pentecost, we celebrate the Holy Spirit, Jesus' gift to us. The Holy Spirit brings us peace.

 ## Try This

Peace be with you.

Trace over the missing letters to complete the sentence.

Read together Jesus' words to his friends.

Jesus Our Light Is Good

Mary and Joseph took Jesus to the Temple. Simeon, a holy man, thanked God for sending Jesus. He called Jesus a light for the world.

Based on Luke 2:32

 ## Try This

Trace over the letters and color them.

Thank Jesus for being a light for the world.

Mary Is Good

Mary is the mother of Jesus.

She is our heavenly mother.

We celebrate her birthday on September 8.

 **Try This**

Color and decorate Mary's cake.

Wish Mary a happy birthday.

Saint Joseph Is Good

Joseph took care of Jesus and Mary.

Joseph was a good man.

Jesus helped Joseph.

 Try This

Draw something that Joseph and Jesus might have built together from wood.

The Holy Family Is Good

God chose Mary to be the mother of Jesus. God chose Joseph to be the foster father of Jesus.

Jesus, Mary, and Joseph cared for one another. They are called the Holy Family.

Try This

Draw a picture of your family.

The Feast of the Holy Family in Families

Yours Is a Holy Family Too

The feast of the Holy Family is celebrated each year on the Sunday after Christmas. It's good timing. With the birth of Jesus, a family was born too. But this day is not only for Jesus, Mary, and Joseph. By entering creation as an infant, God made all families holy. And while it might be hard to visualize one's own family as holy amid all the comings and goings—the laundry and the dishes, the obligations of work and school, not to mention the inevitable power struggles, misunderstandings, and conflicts—it is true nevertheless. Families are indeed holy. The dictionary defines the word *holy* as "belonging to, derived from, or associated with a divine power." That sounds like the definition of a family! Moreover, there is no better way to learn about ourselves, discover our weaknesses, and develop our strengths than in the sometimes calm and sometimes chaotic rhythms of family life. For this powerful spiritual workout, we can be truly grateful.

Celebrating Your Values with the Holy Family

- In every argument, see the opportunity for reconciliation.

- On every birthday, see the opportunity to celebrate the unfathomably marvelous gift of life.

- In every difficult family situation, see the opportunity to use your imagination and choose a new response.

- In every new experience for your child, see the opportunity to reexperience your own childhood with the awareness of God's grace.

- In every sickness, see the opportunity to show compassion.

One of the ways families thrive is by having a clear identity. Have each family member choose a virtue or characteristic that describes your family as a whole. Create a symbol for each one and together design a crest that represents your highest ideals and aspirations as a family. Mount it where everyone can see it.

Be vigilant about keeping your family traditions. Through their elements of ritual and symbol (however simple), along with the memories they create, traditions act powerfully to keep families working and striving together.

Angels Are Good

Prayer to the Guardian Angel

Angel sent by God to guide me,

be my light and walk beside me;

be my guardian and protect me;

in the paths of life direct me.

Amen.

 ## Try This

Follow the path guided by your guardian angel.

Saint Thérèse Is Good

A picture story

✝ Try This

Ask Saint Thérèse, the Little Flower of Jesus, to help you love God.

Saint Francis Is Good

Saint Francis loved everything God made.

He called all of God's creatures his brothers and sisters.

 Try This

Draw a picture of your favorite animal.

Thank God for your favorite animal.

Saint Elizabeth Ann Seton Is Good

Saint Elizabeth Ann Seton is the first saint who was born in America.

She was kind to others, especially to people in need. We can show kindness to others too.

Try This

Draw yourself being kind to someone.

Saint Nicholas Is Good

Saint Nicholas was a kind bishop. He surprised people with acts of love.

He helped people in need.

✝ Try This

Color the shoe.

Think of kind things you can do for others.

Draw a piece of candy or fruit in the shoe for each thing you think of.

The Feast of Saint Nicholas in Families

Saint Nicholas: Model of Selfless Generosity

The story of Saint Nicholas is full of suspense, intrigue, and mystery. It is the story of three young girls in dire circumstances, their limited choices, and a last-minute anonymous rescue by a generous and holy man.

Legend has it that a man with three daughters fell on hard times. With each passing day the young women's prospects looked more and more bleak. It seemed that their only alternative was to sell themselves into a miserable life of servitude. Upon hearing of their plight, Nicholas, a fourth-century bishop of Myra, in what is now Turkey, secretly tossed a bag of gold into the girls' home on three consecutive nights. On the third night, the grateful father waited in hopes of learning the identity of this generous benefactor. But Nicholas outsmarted him by dropping the bag down the chimney. (We can see how the spirit of this generous man was adapted over time into the story of Santa Claus.)

History is full of stories of people who have been rescued from difficult circumstances. What makes this story so compelling is that the gifts were delivered in secret, under the cover of darkness. Nicholas's only desire was to be helpful, not to be recognized or thanked. And though his act of secret generosity eventually became known, people were inspired by his example to engage in secret acts of generosity and gift giving, even after his death. Saint Nicholas exemplified Jesus' advice to "Keep your deeds of mercy in secret." (Matthew 6:4)

Celebrating Your Values With Saint Nicholas

1. In many cultures children celebrate the feast of Saint Nicholas by putting their shoes near the front door on the evening of December 5 (the eve of his feast day), in the hope that their shoes will be secretly filled with treats during the night, such as gold-wrapped chocolate coins or an age-appropriate book that extols the virtue of generosity.

2. Tell your child the story of Saint Nicholas and have each family member put his or her name on a slip of paper. Then have each person secretly pick one of the names and do at least one secret good deed a day for that person during the following week.

3. Think of someone your family knows who could use encouragement. Send a note saying that you are thinking of and praying for that person and sign it, "Your secret friends." Remember that person in your prayers before meals during the coming week.

Saint Bernadette Is Good

Mary visited Bernadette long ago.

Mary asked for prayers and sacrifices.

We do what Mary asks.

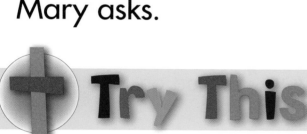

✝ Try This

Color the rays yellow.

Color Mary's dress blue.

Saint Valentine Is Good

Saint Valentine showed his love for others by sending letters. We honor Saint Valentine by sending valentines to loved ones.

Jesus said, "Love one another as I have loved you." Based on John 13:34

✝ Try This

Color the valentine message.

Pray that God will help you love others.

I Love You

Saint Patrick Is Good

A missionary travels to another country to tell people about God's love.

Saint Patrick was a missionary.

He taught the people of Ireland about God.

 Try This

Color the cross.

Pray the Sign of the Cross.

Saint Julie Billiart Is Good

Saint Julie Billiart was a Sister. She taught children to love God.

Sisters have a special love for God. Sisters share God's love with others.

✝ Try This

G ☐ D IS G ☐ ☐ D

Write the letter O in the empty blocks.

Read what Saint Julie taught.

Our Lady of Guadalupe Is Good

Mary appeared to Juan Diego.

She spoke to him.

Mary told Juan Diego, "Ask for my help."

Mary will help us when we ask.

✝ Try This

Color the picture of Our Lady of Guadalupe.

Ask Mary to help you.

Our Mother in Heaven Is Good

During the month of May, we honor Mary.

Mary is our Queen and Mother.

Mary prays to God for us.

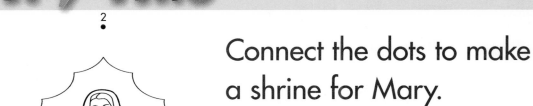

Try This

Connect the dots to make a shrine for Mary.

Color the picture.

Jesus Loves Me

Chapter 1

Chapter 12 ➔

Hail Mary, full of grace.

JESUS

Hail Mary

Hail Mary, full of grace,
the Lord is with you.
Blessed are you among
women,
and blessed is the fruit
of your womb, Jesus.
Holy Mary, Mother of God,
pray for us sinners,
now and at the hour of
our death.
Amen.

My name is

_____

Chapter 3

I have loved you with
an everlasting love.

Based on Jeremiah 31:3

Chapter 5

Chapter 5

Father in heaven,
our hearts desire the warmth of your love;
our minds are searching
for the light of your Word.

Increase our longing for Jesus
and help us grow in love
that we may rejoice in his presence
and welcome his light in our lives.
We pray in the name of Jesus the Lord.
Amen.

Amen

Our Father

Chapter 7 ▼

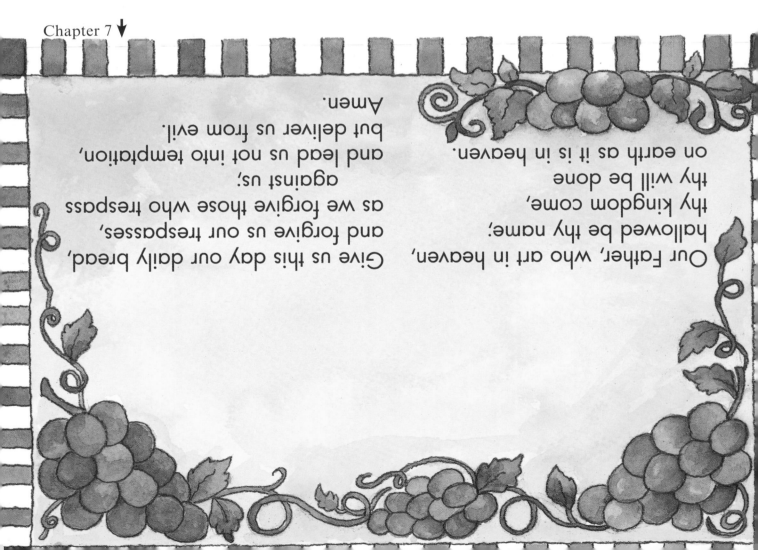

Our Father, who art in heaven,
hallowed be thy name;
thy kingdom come,
thy will be done
on earth as it is in heaven.
Give us this day our daily bread,
and forgive us our trespasses,
as we forgive those who trespass
against us;
and lead us not into temptation,
but deliver us from evil.
Amen.

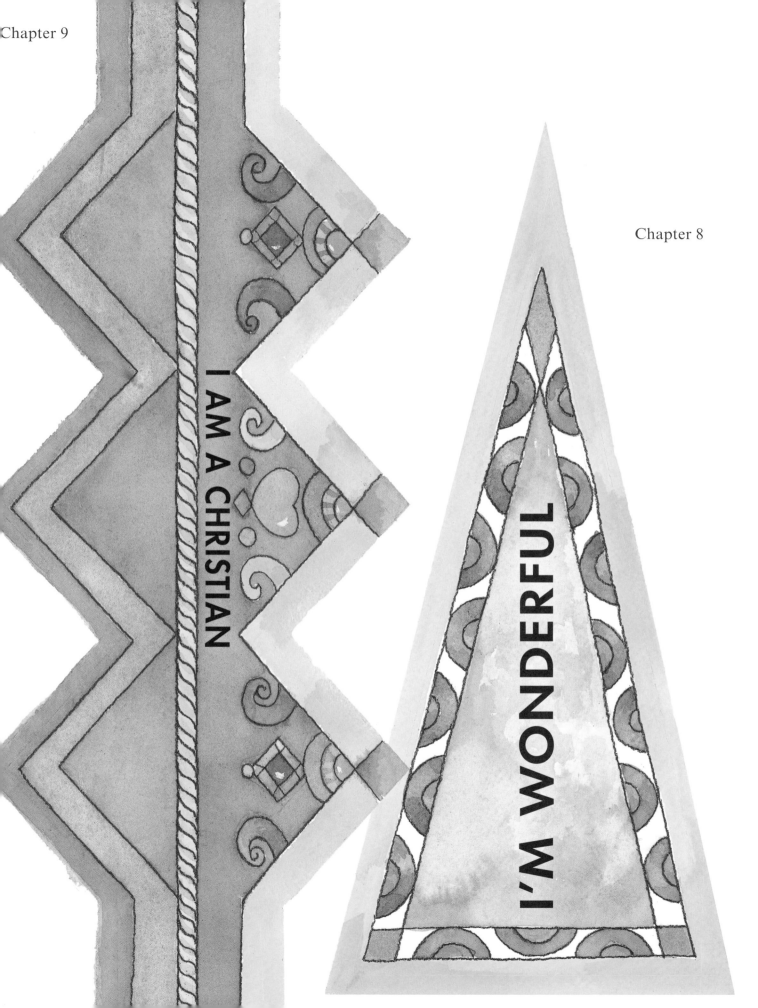

I AM A CHRISTIAN

I'M WONDERFUL

Bless us, O Lord,
and these your gifts
which we are about to receive
from your goodness.
Through Christ our Lord.
Amen.

Chapter 10

Special Seasons and Days,
Lesson 2

Chapter 21

YES

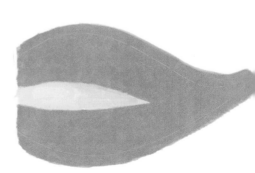

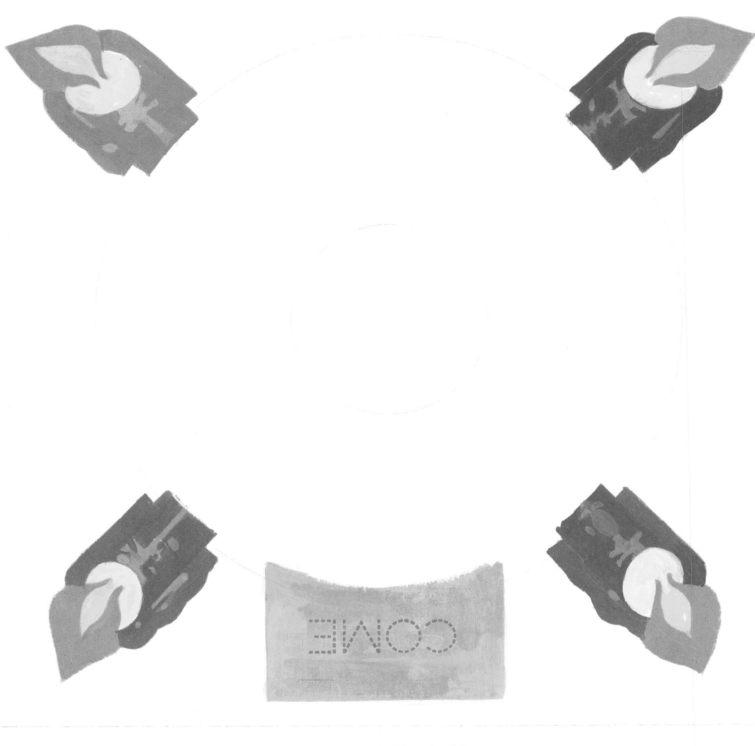

Chapter 12

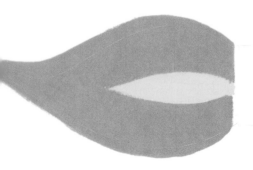

part b

Chapter 13

attach to part b

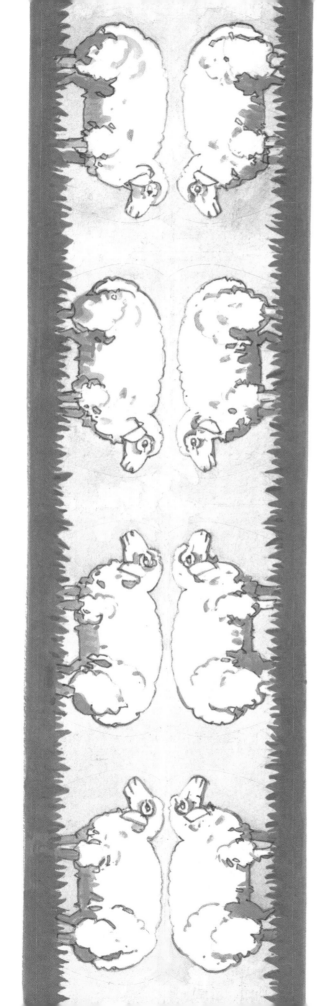

Jesus

Chapter 14

Chapter 16

Chapter 19

ALLELUIA

ALLELUIA

Chapter 20

Chapter 20

Jesus loves us.

Jesus
is
risen!

ALLELUIA

Jesus
is
risen!

ALLELUIA

fold

fold

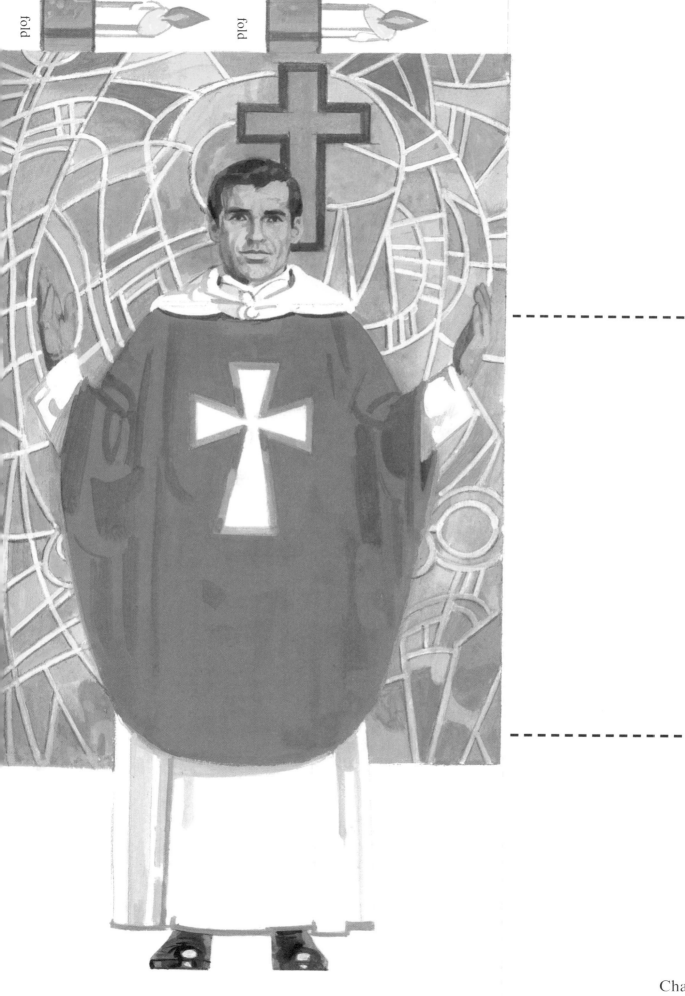